The only REAL
way to sail... is to get
WET!

Happy Father's Day
Dad!

Mark

D1030459

6·15·97

Classic One-Designs

Jack Coote

WATERLINE

Published by Waterline Books
an imprint of Airlife Publishing Ltd
101 Longden Rd, Shrewsbury, England

© Jack Coote 1994

All rights reserved. No part of this publication
may be reproduced, stored in a retrieval system
or transmitted in any form or by any means,
electronic, mechanical, photocopying, recording
or otherwise, without the prior permission in
writing of Waterline Books.

ISBN 1 85310 347 0

A Sheerstrake production.

A CIP catalogue record of this book
is available from the British Library

Acknowledgements

Jack Coote, sadly passed away before he was able to prepare a list of the people who helped with his research into the many classes of boat that are included in this book. As Jack's editor, I was very aware of the tremendous support that he was given by many people from different parts of the sailing world. I have formulated the following list of acknowledgements based on the author's many research files and endeavoured to include those people who have contributed in one way or another to 'Classic One-Designs'. Jack would have wished to thank those listed below and I am sure that there would also be others who are not included; to those sailors I apologise.

The Water Wags, Jim Nugent: *Howth Seventeens*, Bryan Lynch: *Yorkshire OD*, The Secretary, Royal Yorkshire YC, Mr I. Harness — David Armstrong and Ray Ellis: *West Lancashire Seabird*, Jim Morgan, Roger Ryan and Andrew and Linda Read: *Yare and Bure OD*, Michael Evans: *'X' Class OD*, Pamela Rayner: *International Star'*, Richard Munson, Neil MacDonald. Stan Ogilvy and Shery Hughes: *Regensboog (Rainbow) Class*, JJ Kracht and V de Goede: *Sunbeam Class*, Chris Hammock: *St. Mawes OD*, Douglas Barton: *Gareloch OD*, Gordon Mucklow: *West Wight Scow*, Susan Hiscock, Jennifer Nicholls and Mrs MD Davies: *Hamble River Star Class*, Mr MS Robinson: *'Fife' 16ft OD*, John Brooke: *Troy OD*, Tessa Williams and Marcus Lewis: *International 12 Square-Metre Sharpie*, Jan Sanderson and Paddy Spink: *International Snipe*, John Broughton and Thomas Payne: *Norfolk OD 14ft Dinghy*, Paul Janes and Alan Mitchell: *Royal Burnham OD*, Dr AM Basker: *Victory*, Don Metcalf and Nick Chandler: *Hampton OD*, Scott D Wolff and George Webb: *Royal Mersey 'Mylne' OD Class*, Mr CJ Kay: *Loch Long OD*, John Haigh: *Royal Harwich OD*, Bruce Moss and Austin Farrer: *International OD*, John Burnham, BW Walker and Tore Gronvold: *National Redwing*, Dr AG (Jonah) Jones: *International Lightning*, Tony McBride and Donna Foot: *International 110*, Will Craig: *Nordie Folkboat*, David Freeman, Peter Ament and Hans Ogren: *Thistle OD*, Honey Abramson: *National Firefly*, Elizabeth Walker and Jim Bramley: *International 210*, James Robinson: *Aldeburgh Lapwing*, Peter Wilson: *International Cadet*, Gail Nuttal: *International Optimist*, Humphrey Welfare, Mrs Aline Davis and Rick Bischoff.

The photographic content of this work is considerable and involved much research into archives and historic collections. Wherever it has been possible, photographs have been credited in the captions but a further thanks is owed to those whose contributions could not be included.

Peter Hawes, Betty Armstrong, John Tagg, DM Street Jnr, WM Nixon and Robin Gates contributed generally to the research. Tony and Christina Bowers helped in the preparation of the manuscript and finally, Janet Harber, Jack's daughter, was not only of great assistance to her father but has been of great help to me in the final publication of this book.

Peter Coles
Editor

Contents

Post Second World War

Introduction

It is easier to define a one-design yacht than to decide when it becomes 'classic'.

In his book 'The Sailing Yacht' , published in 1906, H. C. Folkard wrote :

"By a 'One Class One-Design' is meant a Class of sailing boats or small Yachts all of the same size and design: a form of boat chosen and adopted by the Club which institutes the Class, the object being that one and all competitors in the sailing matches of the Class, shall meet on fair and equitable terms"

This principle of racing yachts on level terms has certainly stood the test of time. When one-designs and restricted classes were first listed in the 1927 edition of 'Lloyds Register of Yachts', there were sixty of them; while in 1980 when the last edition of the Register was published, it included some 250 different classes.

What makes a one-design, 'classic'?

The answer to that question must necessarily be subjective. Most people think of a 'classic' boat as being made from wood; so, even though many long-established one-design classes now permit building in glass reinforced plastic, I decided to include only those that started out by being built of wood.

I also decided to include only classes that were established before or during the first half of this century, with the result that boats in some of the classes are more than a hundred years old, while almost all of the others have now been around for half a century.

My third condition was that I would consider only boats that were still sailing together as a class in 1990.

Apart from International Classes I have not been able to deal with all of the many indigenous classes of one-designs outside the UK and Ireland.

I am aware that even under these limitations, I have probably failed to mention some classes that qualify for inclusion; so I must apologise to anyone who is unable to find a reference to his favourite local one-design. An idea of the complexity of the task can be gained from a letter I received from Peter Wilson, from whom I had sought information on the one-design classes based at Aldeburgh. Peter replied:

"Aldeburgh has, over the years, had more than its fair share of ODs. At the turn of the century it had some Orwell Corinthian ODs, long since gone; these were in competition with, and superseded by the Whitewings which lasted until 1955. The Redwings were a 12ft 6in lugsail dinghy with bamboo spars and a very heavy cast iron plate dating from about 1922. I think that ten were built and they went on until the Junior Lapwings started in 1952. Even by the standards of their time I expect that they were pretty horrible. The Alde 15ft class built by Eversons started in the early 30s and came to an end in the late 50s being superseded by the Alde 16ft designed by Buchanan and built by Wyatt. In fact only four were built, so effectively the Class was still-born. About forty of the 15ft class were built and in a way they were successful although they were very slow.

The Club had a brief dalliance with the Tumlare before the war but they were too expensive for most people. We imported seven of the Garelochs from the Clyde in I think 1937; these went back in 1956 or 57. We had a few Swallows for a while and these were replaced by Flying Fifteens which still continue. The Dragons started soon after the war and they go on. The first Loch Longs appeared in the mid 50s and they flourish. We had a class of Ajax but they gave way to Squibs.

Morgan Giles drew the Lapwing, and built the first boat in 1947. It is just the same as a TEOD or an EOD except of course only 12ft 6in. They were intended as a senior class but with a reduced rig became the junior class as well. The majority of the boats were built by Nunn Bros with a few built by Appleyards of Lincoln for the Ely Sailing Club. They all finished up here. One of the Nunn boats was on show at the Festival of Britain. The last sail number is 73 and both 72 and 73 were built in 1991, one by us and the other by Upson."

The History of One-Design Yachts

Early Rating Rules

Throughout the nineteenth century, yachting was the exclusive sport of rich men whose attitudes to their pastime was reflected in a saying attributed to the Royal Yacht Squadron: 'Nothing less than 30-T must ever race with our burgee'. The 30-T referred to a system of Tonnage Measurement (T.M.) devised by the Yacht Racing Association in 1881; the formula being:

$$\frac{(\text{Waterline length} + \text{Beam}) \times \text{Beam}}{1730} = \text{Tonnage}$$

Therefore the 30-T minimum required by the RYS meant that the smallest yacht they would allow to race with them would have to be a 40- or 50-footer.

This tonnage method of rating yachts led to extremes of design intended to cheat the rule. Yachts were built with very narrow beam, excessive draught and tremendous sail area. The worst example of the 'plank on edge' type that resulted from the tonnage rule was the *Oona* with a waterline length of 34ft , a beam of 5ft 6in, a draught of 8ft and 2,000 square feet of 'canvas'! The *Oona* was wrecked and her designer lost in 1886 while on her delivery passage from Wivenhoe in Essex to Belfast.

In the same year as the *Oona* was lost, Dixon Kemp, author of the many editions of 'The Manual of Yacht and Boat Sailing', proposed a new rule to take into consideration both waterline length and sail area, using the formula:

$$\frac{\text{Waterline length} \times \text{Sail area}}{6000} = \text{Rating}$$

This rule proved reasonably successful, with yachts competing in groups known as 40-raters, 20-raters, 5-raters, 2½-raters, one-raters and even half-raters – a few of which can still be seen racing on the Thames at Surbiton.

But once again designers found ways around the new formula, this time by building yachts with overhanging bows and sterns, so that the effective waterline length increased when the boat heeled, making it faster. Instead of planks on edge, this form of rule cheating resulted in 'skimming dishes', with overhangs amounting to almost as much again as their waterline length. Perhaps the extreme example of this was *Outlook* designed by W. Starling Burgess to be twice as long on deck as on her waterline!

The One-Design Idea

The dissatisfaction that resulted from rule-cheating was expressed in 1906 by H.C. Folkard in 'The Sailing Yacht'. He wrote :

"The introduction of a one-design class is the result of the uncertainty and dissatisfaction occasioned by rules of measurement and rating of the Yacht Racing Association as applied to small racing yachts, the frequent alteration of those rules, and the facilities afforded for evasion, whereby unfair advantages have been gained, coupled with the expense attendant on the short career of a racing-boat under such rules, involving the building of a new boat nearly every year."

In his book 'The Complete Yachtsman' published a few years later Heckstall-Smith wrote similarly :

"Yachtsmen found the shortness of life of a class racer the source of expense and irritation; a man wanted a new boat every year to keep pace with the rapid evolution of the rule. This led to the introduction of what is known as the One-design class system of yacht racing."

He described the new form of sailing as a sport in which :

"A certain number of yachtsmen at a port or racing locality agree upon a suitable design for the yacht they want to build. Then the vessels are built, rigged, and fitted exactly alike. No yacht is allowed to be altered, and the essential part of an arrangement is that all the yachts in the class should sail on level terms and be as similar as it is possible to make them."

The Pros and Cons of One-Designs

As with many good but revolutionary ideas, the one-design concept did not receive universal support; some yachtsmen believing that the scheme would dampen the enthusiasm of the yacht racing fraternity and prevent the development of improvements in design.

Heckstall-Smith even speculated on what might have happened -

"If all yacht racing had been carried on between one-design classes, improvement in design would have come to a standstill, and if the system and no other had been in vogue in 1845 and had continued, we suppose we should still have been sailing Revenue cutters or cod's heads and mackerel tails; or if it had started in 1880 we should have never got further than planks-on-edge; or in 1895 some other fashionable type with a fin keel and sawn-off counter, and so on; and we should never have arrived at the beautiful yachts of 1912 like the 15-metre Vanity, the 19-metre Octavia or the 23-metre cutter Shamrock."

Heckstall-Smith completed his comments on one-designs by saying:

"They will always continue to play an important part in yachting history, affording great sport for a very large community of hard and keen young boat sailers, but they will not take the place of open YRA or international classes as some critics have supposed."

That was written eighty years ago, but is just as true today.

During the intervening years, many famous yachtsmen and designers expressed their support for one-design racing, among them Uffa Fox and Rod Stevens.

In 1937 Uffa was pleading with the RYA –
"to foster and encourage one-design class racing – because the purpose of such a class is to make all the boats, their rigs and sails, as alike as possible, so that a man wins by his superior skill in sailing and the care he has taken to keep his boat in perfect condition."

In the book 'You Are First' published in 1978, Stevens expressed the opinion that :

"Sailboat racing is at its best when done in a one-design class. This is so, it seems to me, because from the time you start manoeuvring for the best position crossing the line at the start to the time you finish the course, you always know where you stand in relation to the other boats in the race. The first boat to finish is number one and gets the prize."

The Nineteenth Century Classes

During the last decade of the nineteenth century several sailing clubs introduced one-design classes. In 1890 the members of the Bembridge Sailing Club thought that –

"A club whose leading feature would be racing in boats of uniform pattern, would be a success."

Their intention was to have a fleet of :

"Club boats, sloop rigged, with rolling jibs and mainsails so as to reef easily. The subscription to these boats being only £1, a member is enabled to have a summer's sailing and cruising for this small sum, and can, if he is a fair hand in a boat, win good prizes. The boats are as near as possible equal and lots being drawn for them before racing, the best man wins as a rule."

A few years after the Bembridge initiative, the Solent Sailing Club also adopted a proposal for the introduction of a one-design class, and in 1895/6, ten boats were designed by H.W. White and built by White Brothers at Itchen Ferry. The Solent One-Design was 33ft 3in(10m) overall and therefore a large boat by comparison with most of today's one-designs, although still relatively small for those days. These boats, the first one-design in the Solent, quickly became so popular that by 1899 it was necessary for the fleet to sail in two divisions.

The Water Wags

In fact this Solent-based class was not the first one-design; that distinction belongs to the Water Wags of Dublin Bay. The first boat in that class was the *Eva*, built in Dumbarton by McAllister from a model made by Thomas B. Middleton, the originator of the class. Middleton really was a pioneer, placing the following advertisement in the 'Irish Times' on September 18th, 1886 -

"It is proposed to establish in Kingstown (now Dun Laoghaire) a class of sailing punts, with centreboards all built and rigged the same, so that an even harbour race may be had with a light rowing and generally useful boat.

Gentlemen wishing to consider the proposition can have full particulars by applying to M 589, this office"

Middleton received no replies to his advertisement, but undeterred, he immediately sent circulars directly to some fifty local yachtsmen. Among other things, the circular said :

"In order to obtain a boat that will sail to windward without heavy ballast and stay without the use of an oar – with a fair chance of winning in an afternoon race round Kingstown Harbour or off Bray – it has been suggested to get a number of punts built 13 feet long and 4 feet 10in beam with the double bow or 'Scotch Stern' and centreboard, each boat built on the same lines and with the same amount of canvas and sail plan if possible.

Already four or five gentlemen have agreed to get one of these boats built, and if the number could be doubled it would be sufficient to secure a good race one afternoon in the week; and if once started would be sure to bring in recruits, and an association could be formed, or the Dublin Bay SC might be induced to form a sub-section for the class under its sheltering wing."

The circular was more successful than the advertisement and in October 1886, a meeting was held at which – 'different models were discussed and finally fixed on and the sail area was carefully calculated and discussed, also the principal other limitations, especially those of the centreboard were settled so

that men might order or build.'

In the Badminton Library series on Yachting (Vol II), Middleton told of the thinking that led to the formation of the first one-design class of sailing craft, and because it is of such great historical importance, I include part of his story here :

"The pleasantest part of a coast to reside on is, perhaps, that which has a sandy beach shelving gently down into deep water, the wavelets ripple, and the little skiff lies half in the water waiting to be stepped into and pushed off. But the waves are not always ripples; they quickly turn first to breakers and then to heavy surf and consequently the boatman must be prepared to deal with such a change when it occurs. First, the boat cannot be left anchored in the open, as she will surely be lost or damaged in a gale. She must therefore be able to take the ground; that is she cannot have a deep keel and she cannot have any weight of ballast in her.

Now, a boat with no keel and no ballast makes, as everyone knows, a bad sailer; in fact she will only run before the wind like a duck's feather on the water. So a little keel of 3in or 4in is generally used and the boat ballasted with sand-bags filled on the beach, or stones, which are emptied or thrown overboard before landing again. This plan has the objection of being very laborious and making the boat very heavy to launch.

It was to improve on this state of affairs on the beach of this description that is to be found at Shankill in the county of Dublin, that the 'Water Wag' was evolved from a Norwegian 'pram' into which a boiler-plate was fitted as a centreboard as an experiment. This novel craft was called the Cemiostoma. She was built in the year 1878, and was a great success; she sailed like a witch, carried a large sail with ease without any ballast save the iron plate, worked well to windward without making leeway, spun round like a top, and when the boilerplate was raised she ran in on the surf, floated in a few inches of water and eventually sat on the strand on her flat bottom.

In order that these boats might have an occasional race between themselves, to preserve the type and to save the expense of outbuilding and the trouble of handicapping and time allowance, it was further arranged that all the boats should be built on the same lines, and the canvas limited to a cruising amount.

The Water Wag Association was started in 1887, to further develop and preserve the principles of the class. Though it was started by boys, several older 'Wags' joined, and as the boat was never designed for speed, the racing was not originally intended to be hard-down serious sport, but more a sort of friendly sail round a course in boats all alike, and that consequently should be all together; but of course skill in working would bring one to the front and make her harder to catch. Hence the rollicking title 'Water Wags', and the institution of a King and Queen, Bishops, Knights and Rooks, to manage the affairs of the club, their chief duties being to get up as much fun and as many jolly water excursions as possible."

The name 'Water Wag' is thought to have originated from the large flocks of wagtails to be seen on Killiney beach from which the original boats were launched.

The new class got off to a good start and by 1880 some twenty Water Wags had been built and Dixon Kemp had given them his blessing, saying – *"This class is the germ of the One Model Club and has well carried out its initial objects viz. restriction on an advantage of a long purse; preservation of selling value of the boat and the combination of a serviceable and racing boat."*

Although the specification and 'limitations' for the first Water Wag were reasonably detailed, they nevertheless proved inadequate; largely because there was no rule controlling building costs so that within a few years the price of a new boat increased from £15 to £28. Some owners choosing to have their boats planked with cedar rather than the cheaper but heavier larch or pine used for the earlier boats.

So, in 1898 a proposal was made – *"that it is desirable to introduce a new model of boat and if sufficient are built, to form a new class."*

One of the early double-ended Water Wags in Dalkey Sound circa 1895.

The New or 'Club' Water Wag

Length Overall: 14ft 3in (4.3m)
Length Waterline: 14ft (4.2m)
Beam: 5ft 3in (1.6m)
Draught: 9in (3ft 6in) – (22.8cm & 1.06m)
Designer: J.E. Doyle
Sail Area: 110sq ft (10.1sq m)
Builders: Various

J.E. Doyle of Kingstown was commissioned to design the new 'Wag' and produced drawings for a 14ft clench-planked centre-board boat with a raked transom stern and a beam of 5ft 3in. The rig was a loose-footed gunter lug with a small jib, making a total sail area of 110sq ft. It is thought possible that Doyle's seventeen-years-old daughter Mamie designed the new boat, because its lines closely resembled those of a 16ft dinghy she had drawn and submitted to 'The Yachtsman' magazine earlier that same year.

This time, specification of the planking was much more precise :

"Yellow pine ⅜ inch thick (finished thickness) 12 planks on each side, including garboard and top strakes. Planks to be laid in clincher fashion and to overlap at least ¾ inch with their full thickness. No plank to exceed 4½ inches in width measured from land to land. Outside lands must not be thinned down, except within 15 inches of transom and hood ends; but an arris not exceeding ⅛ inch may be taken off, as shown on drawing."

Cost of building was also constrained :

"The cost of boat and spars shall not exceed £16, and the cost of sails shall not exceed £2 for the lug, or £3 for complete suit; but the Committee may, with the consent of two-thirds of the boat owners vary from time to time these limitations of prices."

Further argument and discussion took place before it was agreed in January 1890 to instruct Doyle to complete the design. Four members of the Club undertook to build boats – but only after £4 had been withdrawn from the 'Smoking Concert Fund' to pay for a set of moulds.

Over the years the Water Wag Class has had a succession of notable presidents, one of whom, George Henry Jones, won some money on a horse named *Coquette* and in 1909 proceeded to commission Doyle to build him a Wag that was also named *Coquette*. A more recent President, Seymour Cresswell, and his wife Germaine, sailed *Coquette* so well during 1982 that they were awarded Dublin Bay Sailing Club's Newsom Memorial Cup for the most successful boat in the Bay of any class.

Not only were they the first one-design class, but the Water Wags could also claim to be the first international class because they were adopted by a surprising number of countries throughout the world. In the 1895 edition of Dixon Kemp's 'Manual of Yacht and Boat Sailing', it is reported that there were Water Wags in Argentinian, Australian and Chinese waters.

In 1906, six Wags were built in Singapore for the Colombo Yacht Club of Sri Lanka, in 1908 a fleet was started in Brazil, and by the 1920s there was a fleet of twenty Water Wags at the Royal Madras Yacht Club.

Helena, one of the 'new' Water Wags, built by E.Gray in 1968. (Note the tell-tales on both main and jib)

Jack Brennan and Jim Nugent sailing *Pussie*, an early double-ended Wag, to celebrate the very first race for one-design boats in 1887.

Eva the 'mother' of the Water Wags, in Kingstown harbour (now Dun Laoghaire) in 1890 when owned by T.B. Middleton, the founder of the Class.
All the photographs of Water Wags are by courtesy of Jim Nugent

Howth Seventeens

Length Overall: 22ft 6in (6.9m)
Length Waterline: 17ft (5.2m)
Beam: 6ft (1.8m)
Draught: 3ft 9in (1.1m)
Sail Area: 305sq ft (28sq m)
Designer: W.H. Boyd
Builders: Various

The Howth 17-footers, sometimes referred to as 'Boyd's Boats', can rightfully claim to be the oldest one-design keel-boat class in the world, – and they still race in Dublin Bay.

The birth of the class was largely due to the enthusiasm of Herbert Boyd, whose family were prominent founder members of the Howth Sailing Club when it was formed in 1895.

Although there is no written evidence of it, it seems certain that Herbert Boyd, a capable amateur, was also the designer. The Committee had decided that they should replace their 18ft half-raters with a one-design class of boats that would be 17ft on the waterline, half-decked, have an iron keel and be rigged with a mainsail, a jib and a topsail. It is those topsails that still distinguish the Howth Seventeens today.

The first five boats were built by John Hilditch of Carrickfergus on Belfast Lough at a cost of £90 each, including reaching, working, and storm jibs as well as a spinnaker.

Although the weather was stormy and four of the boats had to seek shelter for a time, all of them were sailed the 110 miles to Howth during Easter weekend of 1898.

In 1899 another three boats were added to the fleet; this time built by Already Clancey of Kingstown. The existing boats had proved satisfactory in every way, but they did have iron keels and since the three new owners had decided to fit their boats with lead keels, it was agreed to make the heavier keel standard and the five earlier Seventeens were suitably modified.

It was for some time claimed that the Dublin Bay 21-Footers were the oldest 'intact' one-design keel-boat class. Without wondering too much about the meaning of 'intact', it is known that the Dublin Bay boats were not launched until 1907, some nine years after the first Howth 17s were built. It is also a fact that the Dublin Bay 21-Footers (more often referred to as the Dublin Bay 17s), were the same as the Howth boats. This resulted from the Howth SC suggesting in 1906 that the Dublin Bay SC might like to adopt their 17-Footer design. It may well have been that the Dublin Bay SC accepted the offer as a way of detaching themselves from J.E. Doyle, builder of the New Water Wags and prospective builder of the new class, who was autocratic enough to have declared that he would 'refuse to build except to his own design'.

The Howth 17 *Leila* rounds a mark during an early Class race.
Photo: from the Boyd Collection.

The offer from Howth was accepted and quotations were obtained from five yards – although not from Doyle. J. Kelly of Portrush got the job and he charged £90 carriage paid with a discount of 2½% for a multiple order.

Five boats were built and launched in 1907, and later that year the two fleets raced together at Howth regatta, when of the twelve starters, the Howth boats took the first seven places.

For many years there were more Dublin Bay 21s that Howth 17s, but over the years interest waned at the Dublin club and by 1960 the class was no longer racing there. Since that time all the Dublin boats have migrated back to Howth, where recently there were seventeen – 17s.

The two youngest Howth 17s were built as recently as 1987/8, when the Irish Youth Training Scheme, helped by a contribution of £25,000 from the Howth Sailing Club, sponsored the building of *Erica* and *Isobel*.

It is interesting to consider how a small and ancient class such as the Howth 17-Footers has managed to retain the boats as true one-designs. One answer can be found in the very few changes that have been made to the original design and specification. Substitution of an iron tiller with one made from wood and the raising of the height of the jib halliard block were not matters likely to have raised much dispute. However, there was a suggestion made in 1925 that the jackyard topsail rig should be abandoned in favour of a Bermudan mainsail. Nothing happened. Then, in 1934, a member proposed the adoption of an 'optional' Bermudan rig. Again nothing happened. Finally, just before World War II, the owner of *Eileen* gave her a Bermudan mainsail, but left the mast where it was, thereby causing excessive lee helm. Once again, nothing more happened. So today we can still enjoy the sight of the Howth 17-Footers sailing with the same rig as they had almost a hundred years ago.

Rosemary, with her distinctive topsail. Photo: Jamie Blandford.

Yorkshire One-Design

Length Overall: 25ft 6in (7.8m)
Length Waterline: 18ft (5.5m)
Beam: 6ft 9in (2.1m)
Draught: 3ft 6in (1.06m)
Sail Area: 320 sq ft (29 sq m)
Designer: J.S. Helyer
Builders: Field & Co.

Bridlington, in the East Riding of Yorkshire is sheltered by the sweeping curve of Flamborough Head from chilly north-easterly winds and for that reason it was a popular seaside resort in Victorian times. The Royal Yorkshire Yacht Club, established in 1847, had a wealthy membership and observed much the same rules as the Royal Yacht Squadron, except that they required their members to own boats of at least 20 tons rather than the 30 ton minimum set by the Squadron.

Towards the end of the century this attitude seemed unreasonable to some members of the Club, who decided to form a break-away group with the intention of establishing a class of small one-design boats. To do this they formed another club, calling it the Pirate Yacht Club and sharing a clubhouse in Bridlington with the local Corinthian Yacht Club. The Corinthians had no tonnage rules and did most of their racing in locally-built cobles.

In 1897 the Pirates ordered a batch of eight new boats from Field & Co., of Itchen Ferry, to a design by J.S. Helyar. An overall length of 25ft 6in related to quite a small boat in the nineteenth century but together with a waterline length of 18ft, a beam of 6ft 9in

and a modest draught of 3ft 6in, that was the size of the Yorkshire One-Design.

All the boats were transported from Southampton to Bridlington by rail in June 1898 and they must have caused something of a stir while being hauled through the town to be launched.

Lots were drawn to allocate the boats, but there was never a No 3 because it had been found that under certain conditions of light, a reversed 3 could be seen through the sail as an 8. A considerate and rather quaint rule was established at the outset, namely that 'if a yacht starts in any race single-handed, the other competitors are to be informed of this, and in such case no spinnaker or reaching foresail may be used by any competitor'.

But such Edwardian courtesy did not survive!

It was only a matter of time before the owners of long established one-design class boats such as the Y.O.D. would begin to question the wisdom of retaining the rig under which the boats were first sailed. In many cases – the Howth 17s are a notable exception – a decision was eventually made to allow conversion from the original gaff or gunter rigs to Bermudan, or as it used to be known, the Marconi rig. In the case of the Yorkshire ODs the rule change came as late as 1973 and then only after an experiment had been conducted by using a cut down wooden mast from a Dragon in *Yilt*, No. 5 in the fleet. The trial quickly showed that under her new rig, *Yilt* was able to beat all the other boats and that meant the end of gunter-rigged Yorkshire ODs. New mainsails were necessary, but the old headsails were retained and fortunately at that time many Dragons were changing to metal spars, so their old wooden masts were going cheaply.

The Dragons were indirectly responsible for the further modernisation of the Y.O.Ds, because after No 9, *Ditherumpop* had been given a Dragon-style cuddy and new Borrensen fittings, most of the rest of the fleet followed suit. But the hulls remained unchanged and very soon the Class will be celebrating its centenary.

Iolanthe sailing from her mooring into Bridlington Bay, before the Class changed its rig. Photo: Arthur Dick

Iolanthe being towed through the streets of Bridlington circa 1920.
Photo overleaf:
Saint sailing off Bridlington. Note the Bermudan rig and Dragon-style cuddy.
Photo: Ray Ellis.

West Lancashire Seabird

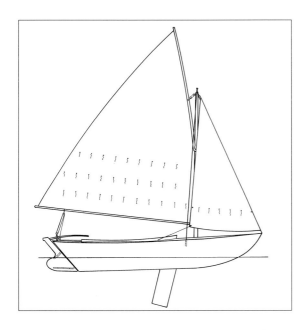

Length overall: 20ft (6.1m)
Length Waterline: 16ft 4in (5m)
Beam: 6ft (1.8m)
Draught: 1ft 4in (4ft 7in)
- (0.4m & 1.4m)
Sail Area: 200sq ft (18 sq m)
Designers: H.G. Baggs and
W. Scott-Hayward
Builder: R. Latham

The Seabirds of the West Lancashire Yacht Club, were established in 1898, at about the same time as the Howth 17s, but they are not to be confused with either the Solent Seabirds or the Seabird Class of the Royal Tay Yacht Club, both of which were quite different boats that came a year or so later. The original Seabird was a 20ft carvel-built, gunter-rigged, inside-ballasted centreboard sloop. The design was the joint work of the Club's Commodore, W. Scott-Hayward and Herbert Baggs, a member. These boats, eight of them at first, were built by R. Latham at Crossens Sluice, just to the north of Southport.

Seabirds could have raced as half-raters, but they almost always competed as a one-design class. The specification set a limit of £35 for the complete boat and in the event, Latham charged £34-17s-6d for each of them. As with many other one-designs that followed, the sail area of the Seabird was limited to 200 square feet, although a small spinnaker was allowed in addition. All the boats were named after sea birds. Their first race, held at Southport in June 1899, was won by *Goshawk*, with sail number 2, and she was still racing in 1990. Scott-Hayward was so enthusiastic about the Seabirds that he soon persuaded the Donaghadee Sailing

Club to adopt the class, calling their boats the 'Seashells'. In Scotland the Gourock Sailing Club also formed a class to the same design and called their fleet the 'Gaels'.

During the early years of this century, there was keen annual competition between the clubs, with racing taking place alternately on Belfast Lough and in the Menai Strait, where the Carnarvon Sailing Club adopted the class in 1902, calling their boats the 'Cariads'.

By 1905 it was realised that if all the boats ostensibly built to the original design were to be controlled as a strict class, then some kind of overall authority would be necessary and consequently the 'Seabird, Seashell and Cariad One-Design Association' was formed.

From the outset the new Association made it clear that they would ensure tight control. For example, when a boat-builder named Roberts of Chester, having been given authority to build five Seabirds for members of the West Kirby Club, took it upon himself to build six, he was forbidden to sell the sixth boat as a Seabird, which it undoubtedly was. It was not until 1963, fifty years later that the Association relented and allowed *Sea Snipe* into the class as No. 33.

The Association not only appointed official builders and sailmakers, but all the boats and sails were ordered through the Association before being delivered to the owners. From the time the class was established, very detailed specifications were drawn up and for the most part have been maintained until today. The fact that so many of the boats are still sailing after more than ninety years shows just how successful the construction and choice of materials have been. The keel and stem are in one piece American elm, steam bent to shape. Planking is of ⅝in pitch-pine on 1¾in sawn oak frames spaced at 24in, with two ⅞in by ⅝in bent timbers between. The boats would carry 560 lbs of moulded iron pigs as internal ballast. Originally the centreplate had to be cut from 'good Bessemer steel', one of the few requirements that were later relaxed, although a recent attempt to use stainless instead of galvanised mild steel was quickly over-ruled. No mechanical 'gadgets' such as sheet winches or rigging screws have ever been allowed on a Seabird; even the positions of the foresail sheet leads are precisely fixed and no fore and aft adjustment is permitted.

It was not until 1965 that a concession was made to allow Terylene sails, which had to be obtained from R. Perry and Co., one of the originally approved sailmakers back in 1908.

In 1910, the Donaghadee Sailing Club wanted to sell its eleven Seashells and the committee of the West Kirby Sailing Club bought the lot. The club then sold them to their members on a first come first served basis, with the proviso that the names of the boats would be changed from seashells to seabirds.

By the time racing was suspended at the outbreak of the 1914 War, some forty Seabirds had been built, but because they were no longer racing on the Clyde, at Belfast or at Carnarvon, it was decided that the Association should delete the names Seashell and Cariad from its title.

After World War II, the class flourished again and a number of new boats were built, one of them by Sam Bond at Rock Ferry, where the progress of her construction was recorded by Brian Ward by a series of excellent drawings in 'Yachting Monthly'. The latest Seabird, *Herring Gull*, was built in 1969, but by 1990 it was estimated that a new boat would have cost more than £15,000.

1989 saw the 90th anniversary of the Seabirds and in the summer of that year, a fleet of them formed the largest class taking part in the Menai Strait Regattas.

Cormorant, Fulmar and *Sea Snipe* racing in the Menai Straits in 1989, the ninetieth year of the Seabird class.

Goshawk, Seabird No 2, under reefed main during the summer of 1899.
Photo: K B Ward (Courtesy of Jim Morgan)

In the short period between the turn of the century and the commencement of the First World War, classes of one-design boats grew rapidly until 1914, when almost all pleasure sailing had to cease.

Early Bembridge Boats

In 1889, a few years before the Redwings, the Bembridge Sailing Club had built a number of 16-foot clench planked boats of 'uniform design' in which members could 'practise boat sailing'. Designed by Capt. E. du Boulay, they were not very attractive craft, with square stems and transom sterns. But their rig was distinctive because it consisted of a combined mainsail and topsail that became known as the Bembridge rig. In 1904 a much better-looking boat resulted from the joint efforts of a member of the Club, E.C. Cockburn, who had won a design competition, and Alfred Westmacott, who was later responsible for several other one-

design boats, including the 'X' class and the Solent Sunbeams.

This second Bembridge boat was 20 feet overall with a waterline length of 15ft 6in, a beam of 5ft 10in, and drawing just 3ft. They were clench planked with an iron keel as well as a centreplate. Sail area was 200 square feet and comprised a gaff main with a roller foresail.

In the 1912 edition of their book 'The Complete Yachtsman', du Boulay and Heckstall-Smith recommended the Bembridge boat for the beginner, adding the advice that – *"Every five years or so it will be advisable to drive out the iron bolts holding the keel and replace them with new ones, which any blacksmith can supply for a few shillings. The old nuts may be used again."*

If the lines of the 1904 Bembridge OD are compared with those of the 'X' OD that came only five years later, it will be seen how alike they are.

Each year during August, the Royal Norfolk and Suffolk YC organise a Sea Week, when the 'Brown' boats race off Lowestoft. Here, *Goshawk* reaches a mark to windward of *Pochard*. Photo: Peter Hawes

Broads One-Design ('The Brown Boats')

Length overall: 24ft (7.3m)
Length Waterline: 16ft (4.9m)
Beam: 5ft 1in (1.6m)
Draught: 3ft (0.9m)
Sail Area: 262sq.ft (24 sq m)
Designer: Linton Hope
Builders: Various

Sailing on the Norfolk and Suffolk Broads was well established by the turn of the century, much of the racing being organised by the Royal Norfolk and Suffolk Yacht Club for Raters and what were known as 'A' and 'B' Class cruisers. But it was the introduction of two one-design classes soon after the turn of the century that greatly increased the numbers of people racing on the Broads. The popularity of sailing grew again after the First World War so that by 1928, 'Yachting Monthly' reported that more than 3,000 yachts had started in races organised by the Broads clubs during that season.

It was in 1900 that a few members of the Royal Norfolk and Suffolk YC decided, against the opinion of some members, that the time had come to introduce a one -design class. They approached Linton Hope, who was already famous for designing *Scotia*, the half-rater that won her class in the Olympic Games of 1900, and asked him to produce a boat that could be sailed without a paid hand under a simple rig that would allow racing at sea as well as on inland waters.

What Linton Hope offered was a 24-foot yacht with characteristic overhangs and efficient underwater lines.

The first five boats were built by the Burnham Boat Building Company in Essex.

Teal (No 3) was bought by E.M. Corbett, who seems to have become the 'father of the fleet'.

The boats were originally planked in cedar, but later in mahogany and when varnished their appearance undoubtedly led to them being referred to as the 'Brown Boats'. Linton Hope gave them a gaff-sloop rig with a total area of 262 square feet. The foresail was tacked to the stemhead and set flying, although later it was hanked to a forestay. The mast was housed in a tabernacle in typical Broads fashion and because of this it was possible to hold occasional 'round the island' races that involved shooting bridges with lowered masts. Several attempts to introduce the Bermudan rig failed because it would have meant moving the tabernacle aft to maintain a balanced helm. Consequently the gaff rig was retained and is still used today.

The seaworthiness of the boats has been proved many times, and it is recorded that in June 1968, when conditions off Lowestoft were bad enough to keep the Dragon fleet in harbour, the Brown Boats went to sea and raced.

At one time the Broads ODs raced annually from Lowestoft to Southwold and back the following day. Here they are seen leaving Southwold harbour in 1973. The three identifiable boats are: *Goshawk* (No.25), *Kingfisher* (No.7) and *Sandpiper* (No.18). Photo: Nick Faulkner; Eastern Counties Newspapers Ltd.

Further proof that the Brown Boats can go to sea was provided in 1956, when a couple of them were sailed from Dover to Calais and back.

Peter Boardman owner and skipper of the re-built *Garganey* described the voyage:

"I suppose we were young and looking for adventure. Our original plan was to take the boats down to Dover by lorry, launch them there, sail to Calais and back and then sail up the coast home to Lowestoft.

We arrived at Dover on 1st June to prepare our boats for the following day's sail to Calais, John Place in Avocet *with Oliver Bridges as crew and me in* Garganey *with Geoff Marjoram. We stayed that night at a transport cafe as that was the only place that would give us a good breakfast early in the morning as we wanted to leave by 7 a.m.*

We actually left at 7.50, one hour after high water, on a course SE by E and reached Cap Gris Nez at 10.20. Our next course was up the coast to Calais where we arrived at 11.50. This was one of the most memorable and enjoyable sails the Brown Boats can ever have had – we had a broad reach in a moderate wind all the way across the Channel and then a run to Calais.

We flew our yellow flags as we entered Calais harbour and looked round for somewhere to moor but we were not met by any Customs Officers or other port officials so moored up and went ashore for lunch. Over lunch we decided to leave our boats in the inner harbour, stay in Calais overnight and then travelled to Paris the next day by train for a couple of nights. We returned from Paris on 5th June by the

24

The 'Brown' boats first appeared on Oulton Broad in 1901 and they were still racing there ninety years later. *Lapwing* (No.22) is in the lead in this shot, taken in 1991. Photo: Paul Janes.

boat train and while all the other passengers went straight aboard the cross-Channel steamer, we had to 'escape' through the goods yard and docks as we had not had our passports stamped on landing.

We decided to spend another night in Calais and sail back to Dover on the following day. The weather was not good and on the morning of the 6th we tried to get a weather forecast on the radio but were unable to find an English station. Avocet, however, had a barometer as part of her equipment and we agreed to make up our own forecast on that. But when her skipper read it, he said: 'Oh! This thing has gone wrong' and promptly threw it overboard!

Eventually, we settled on putting one reef in the sails and sailed at 9.15 a.m. on the high tide on a N by NW course. The wind was very light and we needed full sail but by 10 o'clock it was strong and three reefs were needed. Off the English coast, the tide was against us and we came very close to the South Goodwin buoy while passing between that and the Goodwin lightship.

This was at 2 p.m. but by 3.30 we were safely moored up in Dover Harbour.

And very thankful we were, for this sail must have been the most dangerous a B.O.D. has ever experienced – it certainly frightened me! The waves looked enormous compared with those one sees off Lowestoft but the boats rode them very well. The only water we took aboard was through the tabernacle when the foredeck became submerged."

Almost from the beginning, the Brown Boats attracted the support of two notable families – the Colmans and the Beales and in his history of the Class Charles Goody wrote:-

"In the south-east corner of Oulton Broad was what was known as 'Port Colman' – the boat-house and dyke of Mr Russell Colman, then the outgoing Commodore of the Royal Norfolk and Suffolk Yacht Club, and over the other side of the Broad was the opposition North Bay fleet of Sir John Field, the Commodore-Elect of the R.N.S.Y.C. In these fleets, the Colmans took part that season (1929) in no fewer than 247 races, winning 95 prizes, while the Beales appeared

on the line 262 times and got 82 guns."

Lady Mayhew, née Beryl Colman, was still President of the Class in 1992. In 1986 after several years consideration, the Class Association decided to allow the use of GRP in building boats for acceptance as Broads ODs – 'provided their hulls were indistinguishable in shape, displacement and performance, and as close as possible in appearance to the existing wooden-hulled yachts.'

Paddy Hardiman and David Chrome, who had jointly owned the wooden *Goshawk* (No. 25), had the first GRP Broads OD built by Eastick's Yacht Station at Acle, under the supervision of Neil Hunty, a naval architect. The new boat was named *Merganser* by Lady

Mayhew in 1987, but was not immediately accepted into the Class. Two years later, in 1989, a second plug was made from the hull of *Shearwater* (No. 26), by Kingsley Farrington at Norwich. The first moulding was used to build *Razerbill* by Tony Truman and she was launched in 1990, but she too was not allowed to race in the Class, this time because she had a white hull. In 1991 a ballot was held on whether a white hull was admissible to the Class and although the first vote went against this acceptance, a second ballot accepted a motion that 'any single-colour of topsides' would be acceptable.

By 1992, ten GRP-hulled Broads One-Design boats had been built.

The Belfast Lough One-Design Classes

It could be said that Belfast Lough was a breeding ground for one-design classes. During the first decade of this century there were five classes racing on the Lough, each having its own name: the 'Birds'; the 'Stars'; the 'Fairies'; the 'Gipsies' and the 'Insects'. The first two of these were 30 feet or more

overall and were sailed with the help of paid hands, but the rules of the other classes prohibited any professional crew. The Royal North of Ireland YC, kept a staff of men to look after the boats at a charge, in the case of a 'Fairy', of about £2-10s. for the season.

Iris, one of the gunter-rigged Lough Erne Fairies.

Fairy One-Design

Length Overall: 22ft 6in (6.9m)
Length Waterline: 16ft (4.9m)
Beam: 6ft (1.8m)
Draught: 3ft 6in (1.06m)
Sail Area: 300 sq.ft (287 sq m)
Designer: Linton Hope
Builder: J. Hilditch

The Fairy was designed by Linton Hope in 1901, just after he had achieved fame by winning his class at the 1900 Olympic Games with the half-rater *Scotia*. There are similarities between the Fairy and the Broads OD that Hope had created for the Royal Norfolk and Suffolk YC a year earlier.

The first batch of fourteen Fairies were built by Hilditch of Carrickfergus, who charged £35 each for them, inclusive of spars.

At the time there was some concern that yachtsmen were squeezing boat-builders into producing one-design craft at unreasonably low prices. 'Yachting Monthly' commenting that:-

"When one thinks of such sweated prices one must feel the unfair position of the victims, excellent mechanics many of them, who worked long hours for a bare living. The smaller of them were ever in a state of penury and the larger were not infrequently driven into bankruptcy. It is all very well for a poor man to get a boat to fit his purse – his is a case of needs must – but for comparatively rich men to chivy boat builders into lean contracts and denounce them when they failed to produce the best quality work, was unfair and ungenerous."

The Fairies are planked in pine, and have 15 cwt iron keels and canvassed decks. They were gunter-rigged with a short bowsprit, and were cheap to maintain, as was explained in an article on the Class written for 'Yachting Monthly' in 1914:

"We have kept a very close account of expenditure over a period of six years, and it works out at from £20 to £25 per annum. These figures could be stretched between £15 and £30, according as the boat is neglected or pampered, but £25 will keep the boat in excellent order. The sails, a complete suit, work out about £5-10s., and with ordinary care a suit will last two years. At £5-10s. the temptation is to have a new set every year. The class rules forbid more than one set per annum The boats are worked by three hands, and if these three hands are all owners the expense comes to about £8 per head."

Racing in the Fairies became so popular before the First World War that workmen in the big Belfast shipyards made weekly bets on the results – rather like today's football pools.

In 1905 a second fleet of Fairies was established on Lough Erne and after Hilditch had confirmed that the new boats had been built to Linton Hope's specification, they were allowed to race in the Class. As it happened, the Lough Erne fleet have remained more faithful to the original design than the Cultra boats since their rig has never been converted from gunter to Bermudan, which happened to the Belfast fleet in 1925. As with any one-design class, the R.N.I.Y.C. were faced with the problem of preventing boats being sold away from the club. Their solution was to have the Class Secretary become a trustee for each boat so that a part share was in his name, thereby giving him the right to insist that the boat stayed with the club.

For any class of yacht to survive a prolonged War, it was necessary for someone to make it his business to keep track of the boats during the years when sailing was suspended. In the case of the Belfast Lough Fairies, it was Robert Workman, secretary of the R.N.I.Y.C. who saw to it that all the boats were safely dispersed during World War II. The 'saviour' of the Lough Erne fleet was Walter Cooper, and he made it his business to seek out each boat and buy it if necessary. Such dedication resulted in the post-War resurrection of both fleets of Fairies, one of which still sails under the rig originally designed by Linton Hope in 1901.

Hoylake Opera One-Design

Length Overall: 16ft (4.9m)
Length Waterline: 15ft 6in (4.7m)
Beam: 6ft (1.8m)
Draught: 1ft (2ft 6in)
- (0.3m & 0.76m)
Sail Area: 146 sq ft (13 sq m)
Designer: Alec Latta
Builders: Various

The Marine Lake at Hoylake in Lancashire was opened with a regatta in October 1899. The sailing was organised by the Hoylake Sailing Club and the boats were 12ft centreboard dinghies. Two years later, a break-away group took most of the dinghies just around the corner to West Kirby, where they formed the West Kirby Sailing Club.

Not to be outdone, the members of the Hoylake Club then commissioned a somewhat larger centreboarder from Alec Latta, a local designer. The first of the new boats was delivered in 1902 and was named *San Toy*, the Club having decided that all the boats in the Class should be named after operas. Other boats have been named

Princess Ida, *Carmen*, *Fidelio* and *La Tosca*. The sails of an Opera bear no insignia, simply the Class number of the boat. They are normally sailed with a crew of three.

Latta may have been influenced by the Water Wag because although the Operas are slightly larger, there are similarities between the two designs, particularly in their rigs.

The clench-built hull of the Opera is 16 feet overall and only 6 inches less on the waterline. The hull draws just a foot with the plate up. Unlike the Water Wag, the Opera is three-quarter decked, although the cockpit is very large and the side decking narrow. No drawings for the boat exist and although boats were built by different yards, they all used the original Latta moulds.

The rig of an Opera is interesting in several ways, and although trials were held some years ago with one boat converted to Bermudan rig, no significant advantage resulted and the original rig and sail plan were retained.

The main is a high peaked lugsail with a loose foot and seams running parallel to the leech – as they usually did before the turn of the century.

Of the 146 sq ft allowed, 110 sq ft is in the main and the other 36 sq ft in a tiny jib. To keep the boat exciting to sail, the Opera, like the Water Wag, is allowed a spinnaker. The length of the spinnaker boom exceeds the base of the foretriangle because the mast is so short that the only way a 62 sq ft spinnaker can be set is on a long boom.

Nowadays the highlight of the season for the Class is when they compete during the Menai Straits Fortnight in August.

These two Operas – *Orchid* (No.10) and *Betty* (No.12), are seen taking part in the 1988 Menai Straits Regatta. Photo: William Rowntree.

The Hoylake Opera, *Fidelio*, with all sail set. Photo: William Rowntree.

'Waverley' One-Design

Length Overall: 18ft (5.5m)
Length Waterline: 14ft 6in (4.4m)
Beam: 6ft (1.8m)
Draught: 2ft 9in (0.8m)
Sail Area: 200 sq. ft (18 sq m)
Designer: J. Wylie
Builders: Various

A year or so after the Fairies were established at the Royal North of Ireland YC, the County Antrim YC at Whitehaven, only a few miles from Cultra, decided that they too would have a one-design class of their own. The boats became known as the 'Waverleys' because they were all named after some character or place from Scott's novels.

John Wylie, a physics lecturer at Queens University in Belfast, designed the Waverley; an 18ft gunter-rigged, carvel-planked, transom sterned keel boat with a beam of 6ft and a draught of 2ft 9in.

The first three were built in 1904 for £27 each. One of them, *Talisman* was owned by Wylie himself, who proceeded to demonstrate the seaworthiness of his creation by cruising to the West Coast of Scotland and back with his wife as crew.

By 1907, eight boats had been built and were sailed at Whitehaven, then, in 1912 the Ballyholme YC became interested in the

The Waverley Class, *Fair Maid* on Belfast Lough. Photo: Betty Armstrong.

Class after one of their members had bought the Waverley. For many years after that the Whitehaven and Ballyholme boats raced against each other.

Just before the first World War, the County Antrim YC allowed the Strangford Lough YC to build to the lines of the Waverley, although the six new boats were originally known as the 'Dancers'. Unfortunately most of the 'Dancers' were lost in a gale that struck Belfast Lough in the 1950s.

The Class was in the doldrums for some years after that, but by 1960, four boats were racing again at Ballyholme and from that time numbers increased until some ten Waverlies were competing there in the 1980s. The rig of the Waverley is now the same as it was originally, although for a while in the late 1930s, Bermudan and gunter-rigged boats did race together.

West Kirby Star

Length Overall: 16ft 9in (5.1m)
Length Waterline: 16ft (4.9m)
Beam: 5ft 6in (1.7m)
Draught: 1ft 6in (4ft)
- (0.45m & 1.2m)
Sail Area: 160 sq ft (15 sq m)
Designer: G. Cockshott
Builder: R. Latham

This class, like the Seabird, was established by the West Lancashire Yacht Club in 1906, when the Club decided that besides the Seabird, they needed – 'a new inexpensive class of boat, intended for their younger and less experienced members'. To make sure that the intention was met, one of the rules of the new class prohibited – 'any past or present helmsman of any local class from steering a Star class boat in any West Kirby race'.

The Star, designed by George Cockshott, is a tough, gunter-rigged half-decked clench-built boat with an overall length of 16ft 9in and a draught of only 18 in with its iron centreplate up. They carry 5cwt of internal ballast and all have red sails with a distinguishing number in black within a white star. The West Lancashire Club kept their fleet of Stars until 1922 and then sold them to the West Kirby Sailing Club, who held a ballot to decide which of their members could buy one of the transferred boats, provided they agreed never to offer the boats for sale outside the Club.

The Stars proved popular and by 1950, some seventy boats had been built, although by 1981, when the last two were built, the cost had increased from the original £32 to £4,000.

The West Kirby Star Class rules have always allowed spinnakers, albeit of a modest area. This Star is *Sirius*. Photo: William Rowntree.

It is interesting to speculate on how it came about that so many one-design classes originated on the eastern shores of Ireland and the north-western area of England.

Before the First World War, there were concentrations of yacht racing around Dublin and Belfast, and clubs at Lytham, Southport, Mersey, Hoylake, Rhyl, Llandudno, Beaumaris, Bangor, Menai, Dinowic and Carnarvon. Perhaps it was the prosperity due to shipping and shipbuilding in those areas that led to such early enthusiasm for small boat sailing.

Yare and Bure One-Design Class

Length Overall: 20ft (6m)
Length Waterline: 18ft (5.5m)
Beam: 6ft (1.8m)
Draught: 2ft 9in (0.8m)
Sail Area: 275 sq ft (25 sq m)
Designer: Ernest Woods
Builder: Ernest Woods,
Herbert Woods, Kingsley Farrington.
Portsmouth Yardstick: 114

In 1908, one year after the Yare Sailing Club had joined forces with the Bure Sailing Club, the new club introduced the Yare and Bure One-Design class, a somewhat smaller keel boat than the Broads OD, introduced by the Royal Norfolk and Suffolk Yacht Club a few years earlier. The members of the Yare and Bure SC were probably not as affluent as those who paid their two guineas annual subscription to the Royal Norfolk and Suffolk. Nevertheless, some members of the Yare and Bure Club, led by a Mr Clark, thought that they too should have their own one-design class. The idea was turned down by the Committee of the day, but Clark and his supporters won approval of the members at a special meeting and in 1908 Ernest Woods of Cantley designed and built the first boat – charging £57-10s for it.

Although shorter overall, the Yare and Bure OD is slightly longer on the waterline than the Broads O.D. The 'White Boats' as they are known locally, were carvel-planked with a transom stern and more beam than the B.O.D.s. They are gunter-rigged sloops with an unusually large sail area of 275 square feet. One boat – the *Privateer* sailed for a while with a mainsail of 350 square feet and a jib of 125 square feet. Needless to say she had to race outside the class, but she did clean up in races around the Broads. The Yare and Bure boats have no identifying insignia on their sails, simply the boat's number. At first all the Yare and Bure ODs were named after butterflies, but when the supply of names ran out it was agreed to use the names of moths as well.

The hundredth boat was built in 1981, the year in which it was decided to allow GRP construction. Since then Kingsley Farrington of Norwich has been producing hulls that are layed up in a mould taken from No. 15 – the wooden *Butterfly*.

HRH The Princess Royal at the helm of *Alder Willow* during the celebration of the 80th anniversary of the Yare & Bure OD Class.

Willow Beauty, the Yare & Bure OD on Wroxham Broad in 1981.

'X' Class One-Design

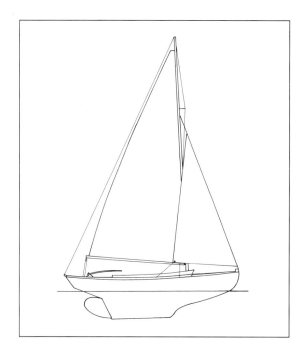

Length Overall: 20ft 8⅜ in (6.3m)
Length Waterline: 17ft 6in (5.3m)
Beam: 6ft (1.8m)
Draught: 2ft 9in (0.8m)
Displacement: 2875lbs (min)
(1302kg)
Sail Area: 210 sq ft (19 sq m)
Designer: A Westmacott
Builders: Various

It seems surprising that such a famous sailing boat as the 'X' One-design should have been introduced by a club that was primarily interested in motor-boats. The Motor Yacht Club was founded in 1903 with Lord Montague of Beaulieu as its Rear Commodore and most of the early members came from the world of engineering. The Club was based on board an old Admiralty survey ship named *Enchantress*, moored off Netley on Southampton Water. From the outset there must have been an interest in sailing because the club had a number of 18ft open centreboard dinghies and in 1909 it was decided to replace them with five small boats of the type that Arthur Westmacott had designed for the Bembridge OD Class in 1904. The boats were to be built by Woodnutts of St. Helens, for whom Westmacott worked, but instead of being clench-planked with centreplates like the Bembridge boats, the M.Y.C. boats were carvel-built and had iron keels. The new boats cost £48-60 each, but this was after Woodnutt's had made a small allowance on the 18-footers they took in part exchange.

Several members of the Club ordered boats for themselves so that by the time the First World War commenced some ten of them

had been built. During the War the club boats were all stored in a boat-house, but their sails and gear were left aboard *Enchantress* which was towed to Southampton and used as headquarters of the R.N.V.R. before being burnt out just before the War ended.

After the War, new sails and spars were made and the club sold its boats to individual members and also obtained a licence from Westmacott to allow yards other than Woodnutts to build to the original design.

Then in December 1921, an interesting letter from the Hon. Secretary of the Royal Motor Yacht Club (the Club had been granted a Royal warrant by that time), appeared in 'Yachting Monthly' under the heading – 'The "Z" OD Sailing Class.' In part it read:

"In these hard times there must be a large number of participators in the exhilarating sport of yacht racing who consider themselves debarred partly by the thought of cost and partly by lack of opportunity; whilst even a comfortable old cruiser, which might have been within the means of many in pre-war days, is now, as likely as not, out of the question owing to the enhanced expenses of crew, sails, gear and practically every item involved.

The varnished hull of *Rooster* suits a boat belonging to a Class that still believes in wood.
Photo: Malcolm Donald.

To meet these difficulties as far as they apply to small sailing yachts, the Royal Motor Yacht Club has decided to throw open its well-known One-design Sailing Boat Class to individual ownership, reserving a nucleus of 'club boats' for the use of beginners.

There are in fact quite a number of these small yachts already in existence, the type having proved popular both in home and colonial waters, owing to its weatherly sea-going qualities, combined with a good turn of speed, whilst there is no record of any of the 87 boats built to date off the original moulds having been capsized or swamped.

The Class will be distinguished by the letter 'Z' on the mainsail over the boat's number, which will be assigned in rotation."

Signed: *C.V.C. Hobart Lt.Col.*

It is not clear just why or when it was decided to change the distinguishing mark of the Class from 'Z' to 'X', but certainly it had happened by 1924, when 'Yachting Monthly' reported that the winner of the race for the Jessett Challenge Cup for the 'X' Class was *Stepaside*, owned by Col. O.W. Carey. *Stepaside* originally called *Mistletoe*, was 'X' OD No 1, and she is now in the Maritime Museum at Poole.

The prototype of the 'X' boat, built by Woodnutts at St. Helens in 1909, continued sailing until 1974, when she was presented to the National Maritime Museum at Greenwich. After Westmacott had agreed to let others build to his design, a number of different yards took advantage of the derestriction between 1923 and 1926, including Newman of Poole, the Berthon

The 'X' OD, *Coquette* when she was gaff rigged. Although the gaff rig was allowed for 'X' boats until 1950, most of the fleet converted to Bermudan soon after it was permitted in 1928. Photo: Beken of Cowes

Boat Company of Lymington and Kemp of Hythe. A total of 23 boats were built by Woodnutts, Newman and Berthon between 1927 and 1929. During the depression of the early 1930s very few boats of any kind were built, but in the latter half of the decade there was a fresh spurt and another 30 boats were completed.

After World War II, the Class thrived once again; Woodnutts building 19 'X' boats, Hampers of Fareham 49, Burnes of Bosham 7, Souters and Lallow of Cowes 3 and 25 respectively. Harrison Butler, the famous amateur yacht designer, once owned what he believed was an 'X' OD, until he discovered that, *Moyezerka*, originally *Schullach*, was in fact one of Westmacott's earlier designs from which a centreplate had been removed and her keel lowered to conform to the 'X' boat's draught of two feet and nine inches.

Despite the conversion, Harrison Butler considered that his boat was in effect an 'X' OD, and in the early 1920s he converted her rig from gaff to Bermudan – several years before that change was permitted in the Class. He also considered that the design of the 'X' boat was excellent – 'and incorporated enough of the racing element to inculcate good methods of sailing and to cultivate a sympathetic touch in going to windward'.

Altogether, eleven different builders have built 'X' boats over the years and so far as the hulls were concerned, the only significant variation allowed was the substitution of the original pitch pine planking by mahogany. Even this option of a lighter wood had to be compensated by the installation of four 15 pound lead weights, precisely positioned in the hull.

The inequality resulting from the fact that some older boats become heavier than recently built boats, has been dealt with by the introduction of a rule requiring all boats to weigh at least 2875 lbs; if necessary by the addition of the same type of lead ballast slabs positioned as required for boats planked with mahogany.

'X' boats are stable enough for the older generation to enjoy sailing them.
Photo: Hamo Thornycroft.

'Dry' sailing is certainly not allowed and a boat – 'must not be out of the water for more than 50 hours in any consecutive 14 days' and to be eligible to race during Cowes Week, – the highlight of the 'X' Boats season – 'a yacht must have been launched prior to July 1st'.

Bermudan rig was allowed in the Class after 1928, and although the original gaff rig remained an option until 1950, most of the racing fleet quickly converted to the taller rig. In 1950 the size of the mainsail was also reduced by using a shorter boom and increasing the size of the foresail. A short boom allowed the use of a standing backstay so that runners were no longer needed.

Consideration has been regularly given to the adoption of metal spars, but since any change of such significance requires a 75% majority support, it has been rejected at least three times so far, and all the 'X' boats in the Class still have wooden spars. Furthermore, so that there can be no doubt about what is underneath, all masts must be varnished and not painted.

Toe straps and trapezes or any apparatus – 'the purpose or effect of which is or may be to support or assist in supporting a member of the crew outboard or partially outboard is prohibited'.

Echo sounders are not permitted and any sounding must be done with a lead line or a 6ft bamboo cane.

A new 'X' OD may only be built at the yard of a builder approved by the Committee and under the supervision of the Official Measurer. In 1991 the three authorised builders were: Ian Lallow of Cowes, John Perry of Southsea and Ken Latham of Poole.

It is by means of controls such as these that the 'X' Class has maintained its strict one-design character for more than eighty years.

Throughout the long history of the Class, the 'X' OD has been sailed and raced at a number of different centres, where Divisions of the Class have been formed. The first such fleet was established at Southampton soon after the First World War and continued until 1936 when the boats were sold to a Division at Hamble, where there were still some twenty five boats in 1991. The Parkstone Division, formed in 1924 was still going strong after nearly seventy years. The Lymington Division operated for four years from 1927 to 1931 and then there was a gap before the Division was reformed in 1946, thereafter to become one of the largest fleets. Although the Cowes Division was not formed until 1951, the Class has been a keen supporter of Cowes Week since 1925 with as many as ninety 'X' boats competing against each other. Of the many trophies raced for during the Week, the one most coveted is the Captain's Cup, presented by Harry Brickwood in 1930. Harry Brickwood was Class Captain for almost 30 years and his guidance and foresight was largely responsible for the 'X' Boats becoming such a famous One-Design Class.

Although half-decked and only 20ft long, 'X' Boats have made some remarkable voyages. For instance, *Typhoon* X67, was sailed single-handed from the Hamble to Bordeaux and back. The longest recorded voyage (also single-handed) in the 'X' boat *Tiree*, albeit after she had been converted and given an outboard engine, was from Fishguard in Wales to Sardinia in 1974.

There is little doubt that it is the slightly heavy and extremely strong construction called for by Alfred Westmacott's design that makes these little yachts so durable and seaworthy.

Although it is not compulsory, (it could hardly be with nearly two hundred boats in the Class) some have names beginning with an X – such as *Xylotox*.

International Star

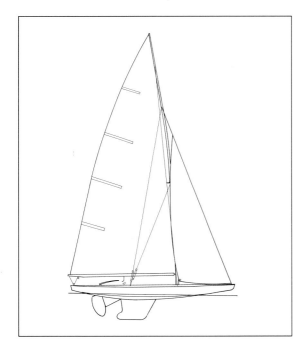

Length Overall: 22ft 7in (6.9m)
Length Waterline: 15ft 6in (4.7m)
Beam: 5ft 8in (1.7m)
Draught: 3ft 6in (1m)
Displacement: 1480lbs (min)
(670kg)
Sail Area: 280 sq ft (25 sq m)
Designer: W Gardner
Builders: Various
Portsmouth Yardstick: 97

It is a remarkable fact that a hard-chine boat designed in the USA in 1910 should still be chosen as an Olympic Class in 1992.

The Star had been preceded by a similar but smaller boat that was sailing from the Manhasset Bay Yacht Club on Long Island Sound in 1906. Those earlier boats were designed by William Gardner, (or at least the design came from his office) and fourteen of them were built and drawn for by lot. The 'Bugs' as they were known, took their names from those of insects and were supposed to be 19ft overall with a beam of 4ft 7in. They were built by Isaac Smith of Port Washington and were to cost $100. But the story has it that 'Ike Smith had a big batch of 18ft planks, so those first Bugs came out nearer 18ft long than 19ft'. To save money, the keel was just an iron plate bolted to the hull. The first time a bug went sailing, it capsized, although because of her very small cockpit, she did not fill. A heavy iron bulb was then added to the bottom of the iron plate fin keel and this was where Smith made up his deficit by charging $40 apiece for the revised keels. There could be no objection, since the original specification said nothing about the weight of the keel.

George A. Corry, Commodore of the Manhasset Bay Yacht Club, had been the moving spirit behind the Bugs, but after racing in them for five years he and some of his friends decided that the Bug was – 'too small and uncomfortable to become popular as a serious long-term proposition'. So they went back to William Gardner and asked him to produce a design of the same type but a bit larger than the Bug. At first the intention was to name the new class the 'Big Bug', but fortunately someone, possibly Stuyvesant Wainwright, suggested the name 'Star'.

The lines of the Star were drawn by Francis Sweisguth of Gardner's office and although the idea for the new boat undoubtedly originated from experience with the Bug, Sweisguth has said that – *"I started from scratch, without ever looking at the Bug lines"*.

An order for 22 Stars was placed towards the end of 1910, the builder being the same Isaac Smith of Port Washington, who this time charged $250 each for them. The boats were ordered by members of clubs at Port Washington, New Rochelle and Rye, so that interclub racing soon began. George Corry's purpose in forming the Star Class has been outlined in Edwin Schoettle's book – 'Sailing Craft' –

"George Corry conceived the idea of providing an inexpensive boat, that was a real little racing machine, for men of ability but moderate means. This was in the days of the large yacht, when racing was a rich man's game and something of a society function as well. Small boats were considered playthings for boys, but it is well to note that from the beginning the Star was never intended as a training school for novices. It was dedicated to experienced skippers who could not afford large yachts."

The January 1911 issue of the 'Rudder' carried drawings of the Star and reported that 'over thirty of the class have been ordered'. The first race between Stars was held on May 30th 1911 at the Harlem Yacht Club. Five boats competed and George Corry won in Star No. 7.

Corry became quite famous as a Star helmsman; the 'New York Sun' reporting in July 1912, that – *"The racing in the Star class is more exciting than with the larger boats. These small craft are handled by youngsters mostly and their ambition is to outsail George Corry in the* Little Dipper".

George Elder first sailed a Star in 1914, and thereafter devoted his time to building the Class into first a national and then international organisation. It was Elder who arranged the meeting in New York in 1922 at which it was agreed to form the 'Star Class Yacht Racing Association'. Each boat had one vote and the annual subscription was $1. The five fleets constituting that first Association were based on the Eastern Long Island Sound, Lake Erie, the Detroit River, Narrangansett Sound and Western Long Island Sound. George Corry was made president of the new Association, but it was George Elder, as secretary, who did the work and continued to do it for a quarter of a century thereafter. By all accounts Elder was an administrator par excellence, and in 1948, fearing that his successor might not maintain his standards without guidance, he wrote a hundred page 'Office Manual' and in the preamble he offered this advice – *"Throughout the year you will get requests for rulings on many strange points. If in doubt, the answer should always be no. If you say no you can never be wrong,* *but if you say yes and are not absolutely positive, then you can let yourselves in for no end of trouble".* According to the first set of rules, drawn up in 1918, the dimensions of the Star were : length not exceeding 22ft 7in. Beam not less than 5ft 7½in. For the rest, everything depended upon a clause which read: *"All measurements and principles of construction and design must be in accordance with the Gardner specifications"*

The waterline length of a Star is 15ft 6in, so there are overhangs at bow and stern and the rudder, in a trunk, is hung behind a small skeg. Although the Star is hard-chined, its bottom is curved aft of frame 3, and after 1965 a set of four templates were used to ensure that the correct radius of curvature had been used by the builders.

Until the 1960s, there had been no weight specified for a Star and it was found that differences between boats could be as great as 200 lbs. It was then agreed that a minimum weight of 1460 lbs would be applied to both wooden and GRP boats. That minimum was subsequently increased by 20 lbs when air bags or other forms of buoyancy became compulsory.

Stars were originally gaff rigged and the size and shape of the mainsail and the jib were defined by sets of four and three dimensions. No more than one suit of new sails per season was allowed. Spars had to be solid and although whisker poles were used, spinnakers were and still are not permitted. Before 1926, apart from boats competing in international events, there were no Class measurers and no certificates were issued. Until then it had been assumed that all 400 of the Stars already built conformed to the designer's specifications. At that point, Adrian Iselin proposed a programme to measure all existing boats and in little more than a year, this had been done. Only one out of the first forty boats to be measured, required any modification.

The 'Marconi' or Bermudan rig was first tried in a Star by D.H. Cowl in 1918, who at William Gardner's suggestion, used a curved hollow spar. That attempt seems to have been a failure and it was not until 1921 that further experiments led to the Bermudan rig being successfully adopted by a Star of the Manhasset Bay fleet. The conversion was

Argus, Star No 4, circa 1911. Photo: Rosenfeld

This photo was taken in the Gulf of La Spezia in Italy, circa 1938. The boat carries the 'flexible rig' innovation developed by Walter von Hutschler.

Although Colin Ratsey had won an Olympic Silver Medal in a Star in 1932, there were only two small fleets of Star Class boats in the U.K. One was on the Solent, where this photograph of *Honey Lamb* and *Starlight* was taken in the 1950s. Photo: Beken of Cowes.

unofficial, but this did not prevent other owners from following suit and before long, the gaff-rigged Star had virtually disappeared. Because of the high peaked gaff that had been commonly used, the change did not necessarily involve buying a new mainsail.

By 1928, when there were some 550 boats in the Class, there was a demand from some countries, particularly France, to modernize the rig of the Star, which despite its low cut Bermudan rig, certainly looked out of date. 'Why build a boat with a 20-year-old rig?' the French asked. 'With a new rig the Star would be popular all over Europe'.

In 1929 the rig was changed, this time requiring a shorter boom and a much taller mast, although still retaining 280 square feet of sail. The Association actively supported this conversion and published a broadsheet with a photograph of a Star under the new rig accompanied by such positive statement as: *"The adoption of the modern rig has given us a rejuvenated Star, a yacht that compares favourably with the newest class and is bound to appeal. We are doing what others have failed to do, retaining the interest of old members and attracting new ones by keeping pace with the times. This policy is essential to the continued world-wide development and success of the Star Class".*

During 1930, the new rig was optional, and as always when a change is made, there were some objectors, so when in the last race of the International series that year, the only two boats using the old rig finished first and second, the doubters seemed to have a point. But very soon, skippers learned to feather their mainsails when working to windward in a strong breeze and then they found they could beat any boat with the lower rig.

Conversion to a tall Bermudan mainsail had the desired effect and new fleets of stars were established in many countries so that 137 boats were added to the Class in 1930 and another 87 in the following year.

Just how the Star came to be included in the 1932 Olympic Games is not clear, because the original intention had been simply to stage a series of races by way of a demonstration in the hope that the Class would be accepted for the 1936 Olympiad. The decision to include the Stars in 1932 was only made late in the previous year, but even so, seven nations were represented. The Gold medal winner was Gilbert Gray of the USA, with Colin Ratsey of the UK taking the Silver and Gunnar Asther of Sweden the Bronze.

With the one exception of 1976, when the Tempest temporarily replaced it, the Star has remained an Olympic Class since 1932 and Gold medals have been won by helmsmen from Germany; Italy; the USSR (2); the Bahamas; Australia; the USA (3) and the UK.

Many famous helmsmen have raced in Stars, including: Tom Blackaller, Dennis Conner, Briggs Cunningham, Paul Elvstrom, Skip Etchells, Walter von Hutscher, Stuart Jardine, Lowell North and Colin Ratsey.

Paul Elvstrom who won the World Championship at Kiel in 1966, always enjoyed sailing a Star, as is evident from his account of a planing run in strong wind:

"Oh! lovely, lovely, planing with the Star with that huge sail. In competition with other Stars it is wonderful but you need a special technique and the main thing is you must trust your rudder because you must not be afraid to break the rudder. If you are scared of breaking the rudder in the Star in strong winds you can't get planing. The main secret of my fast planing in Kiel and other places was that I think I'm harder with my rudder, although the sail also has to be nice and full. But I think most people are afraid to break the rudder. They think they will break the boat but it is the only way to keep it going but when you pass a critical point and get more and more speed then the pressure on the tiller becomes less and less but if it starts to luff up you must never let it go up like you can in a dinghy. If the Star luffs up and the wind disappears from the front of the mainsail, then you are finished. Of course you must not be afraid of the boom breaking either."

Following acceptance of the taller rig, the next major change was the introduction of the flexible or 'bendy' mast, for which Walter von Hutschler was responsible.

Von Hutschler who was born in Brazil of German parents, did not sail a Star in the 1936 Olympic Games, but he did coach Peter Bischoff of Berlin, who proceeded to win the Gold medal in the Class. The following year von Hutschler, crewed by Joachim Weise, won four races at the Star World Championship using the flexible rig in a boat called *Pimm*. The Americans were so taken aback by the new idea that their initial reaction was to have 'bendy' masts declared illegal. Fortunately the objection was rejected and it was not long before flexible masts were the norm in Stars and some other classes.

Although sail tuning by means of flexible spars seems ordinary now, the idea was not so obvious in the 1930s, as von Hutschler reminds us :

"I experimented a lot with different baggy mainsails and in a lucky moment, when the boat was beating to windward without any speed into fairly wild waves and I was standing alongside the mast, I observed the faint curving of the mast, which augmented and diminished the amount of draft in the sail. This gave me the idea of creating a mast that I could flex to match my idea of the best curving according to the sail's bag and the amount of wind. So this was the hour of the birth of the Flexible Rig. It took some time to arrange for the different best angles of the stays and the fore-and-aft mast position, but the final result was a big success. In a short time this rig spread. This was my greatest contribution to the sailing world as it became also adopted by larger boats, although there in much smaller proportion."

Although remembered mainly for his flexible rig, von Hutschler was also first to use a tiller extension in a Star, an extremely valuable device when both helmsman and crew are lying prone along the weather deck.

After the Class had accepted flexible spars, its next major task was to deal with the rapidly growing interest in glass fibre construction. By the early 1960s, all new one-design classes were being built in GRP, and some Star class members, particularly those of the Newport Harbour fleet in California, felt that the Association should allow Stars to be built by this new form of construction.

So, in 1965 specifications were submitted to the Technical Committee and the work had been so well done and the argument was so convincing that the project was

Despite relatively small UK interest in the Star Class, Mike McIntyre and Philip Bryn Vaile won the Olympic Gold Medal in the Star Class at Seoul in 1988.

approved and then confirmed by a vote of the whole membership. The first 'glass' Stars were built by Eichenlaub in California and Lippincott in New Jersey.

For some years after the introduction of GRP hulls, older wooden boats still managed to win races, but gradually the better skippers bought GRP boats because of their easier maintenance. The same changeover happened in the Dragon Class, and in both cases there were traditionalists who lamented the trend.

Inevitably when GRP construction is used for one-design boats, there comes a time when questions are asked about the distribution of weight throughout the hull. It is possible during the laying-up of a GRP hull to concentrate material amidships and low down and to skimp the material used in the ends of the boat. One way of checking the uniformity of lay-up is to cut samples from different places in the hull and deck, but because this perforates the boat it is never popular with either the builder or the owner. In the case of the Stars, this led to an attempt to apply a 'swing test' that would show up any significant departure from normal distribution of weight. But the Star's heavy bulb keel, located as it is away from the centre of gravity of the boat, made the swing test procedure unreliable. After that the Technical Committee decided that the construction of hulls with light ends should be considered self-limiting since – 'if ends are made any lighter they would fall off.'

By 1990, almost eighty years after the Class began, more than 7,500 boats had been built and the Star had once again been chosen as one of the five Classes for the 1992 Olympiad. Surprisingly, although the Gold medal in the Star Class at the Seoul 1988 Olympic Games was won for the UK by Mike McIntyre and Philip Vaile, the Class has never been popular in Britain. This is usually explained by the fact that the mainsail of the Star is extremely large and not well suited to deal with the squalls that sometimes reach gale force even during the summer months around the coasts of Great Britain.

Thames Estuary One-Design

TE

Length Overall: 18ft (5.5m)
Length Waterline: 16ft 9in (5.1m)
Beam: 6ft (1.8m)
Draught: 10in (4ft 9in)
- (0.24m & 1.4m)
Displacement: 1742lbs (789kg)
Sail Area: 210 sq ft (19 sq m)
Designer: Morgan Giles
Builders: Various

Essex One-Design

E

Length Overall: 18ft (5.5m)
Length Waterline: 16ft 9in (5.1m)
Beam: 6ft (1.8m)
Draught: 10in (5ft)
- (0.24 & 1.5m)
Displacement: 1864lbs (844kg)
Sail Area: 210 sq ft (19 sq m)
Designer: Morgan Giles
Builders: Various

Estuary One-Design

Length Overall: 18ft (5.5m)
Length Waterline: 16ft 9in (5.1m)
Beam: 6ft (1.8m)
Draught: 12in (5ft 2in)
- (0.3m & 1.6m)
Sail Area: 210 sq ft (19 sq m)
Designer: Morgan Giles
Builder: Thames Structural Plastics

I found that I had to stretch my rules slightly in order to include the Thames Estuary One-Design Class. The 'Tee-Od' as it is always called in the Southend area of Essex, was established in 1911 and although there are now no boats racing that were built to the original design, an Essex One-Design is still competing, and since the E.O.Ds raced together with the T.E.O.Ds for many years, and the fortunes of the two classes were always intertwined, I thought it not unreasonable to include them both under the same heading.

It is true that *Mallard*, the Essex OD that continued to race in 1990, did so in competition with the GRP Estuary one-designs that were introduced to sail together with the two older classes.

From the time the London-Tilbury-Southend railway line (now known as the Fenchurch Street line and often referred to as the 'misery' line) was opened in 1850, more and more people came to live along the north shore of the Thames Estuary between Southend and Leigh-on-Sea, and by the turn of the century three clubs were established to the west of the famous pier. They were the Alexandra, the Westcliff and the Essex

Yacht Clubs. The Westcliff YC introduced a class of 20ft scows based on an American design, but none of the other local clubs adopted it. By 1912 the Alexandra Yacht Club (The Alex), was concerned that the popularity of the 17-foot open boats it was using at the time had been 'marred by the advent of three new boats ingeniously contrived to evade the restrictions, and these have practically swept the board, so that the older boats have no chance in the racing.'

Thames Estuary One-Design
Clearly the time had come to introduce a one-design class, but the special conditions imposed by the drying flats off the Southend shore precluded the use of a keel boat so the choice had to be a centreboarder and quite a tough one at that. A Committee, including some members of the neighbouring Essex Yacht Club was formed, and a design was commissioned from Morgan Giles of Teignmouth, who drew an 18-foot half-decked clench-built boat planked in wych elm with a beam of 6 feet and a draught of 10 inches, when its 1½cwt cast-iron centreplate was retracted. Moveable lead ballast weighing between 1 and 2 cwt. was also permitted.

The Thames Estuary One-Design Class was originally gunter-rigged with a bamboo gaff and a short bowsprit. This photograph of *Santanita II* shows her racing against the first of the National 18-ft Restricted Class the RYA. introduced in 1939.
Photo: Douglas Went.

Sail area was an ample 210 square feet in the form of a gunter rig on either solid pine or bamboo spars. A spinnaker was also allowed and the crew was limited to three, one of whom could be a paid hand.

Several builders were asked to tender for the first batch of ten boats and the order was won by Drake Brothers of Tollesbury, who asked £35-16s each for them, including spars from Morgan Giles and sails from Cranfield and Carter. As the boats were completed, they were towed round, four at a time from the Blackwater to the Thames behind a Tollesbury smack.

The Thames Estuary One-Design soon became one of the best known boats around the shores of Essex and Kent and anyone who learned to sail in a 'Tee-Od' always reckoned he had served a sound apprenticeship.

After the T.E.O.D.'s first season, one of the owners described a day's racing:-

"You wake up with the windows rattling like fury, get to the Club and listen to the club balcony critics who decide that your boat hasn't got an earthly, and then get into oilies. Going off to the moorings you get your feet soaked because the dinghy leaks like a sieve, and you get under way.

Perhaps you get free, if you have had the pluck to get into what at first looks like a loosing position, but soon turns into a winning one when the others have finished their luffing. You fling round the Pier Buoy and with hardened sheets plug to the Low Way, soaked to the skin and with most of the breath knocked out of your body. If your gear has stood it and the boat isn't too full of water you gybe round the Low Way, and with spinnaker set charge like a runaway horse homewards, yawing about and perhaps having to run by the lee for a while with your boom poking a hole in the sky. Then you make your more dead than alive forrard hand give you a spell and you can have a suck at the pipe and a flask, and prepare for the next round, which will be worse than the first, with the strong ebb running."

Some owners used their T.E.O.Ds as camping cruisers, making modest coast voyages. Cyril Wright, who had *Cutty Sark* one of the original ten boats, described a trip he made single-handed from Westcliff to Osea Island and back.

"There was a smart little southwesterly breeze when I started, and by the time I got to the Maplin it was blowing hard with a nasty short sea. I knew I was in for a dusting on the leg from the Knoll buoy to the mouth of the Blackwater, but I was absolutely astounded by the wonderful weather she made of it. Being single-handed, I had plenty to do; not only did my pram dinghy fill three times and have to be bailed out, but I was constantly occupied in reefing and unreefing between squalls. Eventually I fetched Osea at 9.30 at night after twelve hours of strenuous sailing, very much delighted with my little craft."

Essex One-Design

In 1919 the Essex Yacht Club decided that they too would have to replace the 17ft open boats they had been sailing as a restricted class since 1903. Members of the club had a hand in deciding the specification for the T.E.O.D., which they knew had proven successful; but being human, they thought improvements could be made without departing from the boat's basic dimensions.

Morgan Giles was therefore asked to 'go one better' and improve on his design for the Alexandra Yacht Club. In comparison with the earlier boat, the E.O.D. that resulted had a slightly firmer bilge and a wider transom. The weight of her cast-iron centreplate was increased from 140lbs to 225lbs., and the rig was to be Bermudan (Marconi) instead of gunter. The foresail was set on a luff-spar with the means of booming the sail out when off the wind. Although Giles intended a spinnaker to be used as with the T.E.O.D. that sail was never adopted for the E.O.D.

The original specification called for bamboo spars, but in the event hollow wooden spars were obtained from McGruer of Clynder on the Gareloch. Twelve boats to the new design were ordered from the local yard of Cole and Wiggins, with sails made by Turnidge of Leigh-on-Sea. By this time the cost of the boats had gone up to £100.

For a while the new class had the edge over the T.E.O.D.s but it was not long before the older boats began to change their rigs to Bermudan; this time with taller masts than the E.O.D.s, so they were able to turn the tables once again. Racing between the two classes continued throughout the period between the Wars with the highlight of each season being when fleets of T.E.O.Ds and E.O.D.s came from Ramsgate, Margate, Herne Bay, Whitstable and the Southend Clubs to compete in the Burnham Week regatta on the river Crouch. Occasionally, E.O.Ds indulged in cruising, a couple of them even venturing as far as Calais. Ralph Mountstevens recalls that: "In 1932 two E.O.Ds sailed to Calais and back. They were Chantey which I sailed, and Crescendo sailed by Hulford. The weather was very mixed on the way out and freshish N.E. on the return. 'Jack Yard', the 'Southend Standard' yachting correspondent wrote an admonitory article saying 'Now that it has been done once, let no one else try to do it'."

There was a hilarious sequel, when the owners of the Royal Burnham OD at Burnham also decided to have a go. Their wives, however who did not know of the plan, got to hear of it rather belatedly and chased their men in a motor boat and brought them back before they had cleared the River Crouch.

Estuary One-Design

By 1965 the number of E.O.Ds still racing had fallen to fourteen and these were costing more and more to maintain. If the class was to survive it was essential that a cheaper method of construction would have to be used.

The owners of the remaining T.E.O.Ds were facing the same dilemma and at a meeting of members from both classes, in December it was agreed that a combined committee of members from both Clubs should be formed to consider the future of both Classes. That committee made a number of recommendations, the more important being:-

"1) That it is feasible and practical to produce a new boat in fibreglass, whilst preserving the performance and character of the existing boats.

2) That the Classes could and should combine to race together on level terms with existing boats and with new boats built to a composite Class.

3) That a combined Class Owners Association should be formed to govern the affairs of a composite class along the lines

The Essex One-Design was drawn by Morgan Giles in 1919, a decade after he had produced the T.E.O.D. The E.O.D. was Bermudan-rigged from the outset, although not initially with the tall masts and short booms of these boats. Photo: Trevor Davies

The Estuary One-Design, is a GRP boat with the same rig and sail area as the T.E.O.D. and E.O.D., but slightly different bow sections. Here they are seen racing on the river Crouch during Burnham Week in 1989. Photo: Coloryan

of the present T.E.O.D. Association."

These recommendations were accepted and the new Estuary Class of GRP boats was born.

However certain conditions were drawn up to ensure that it would be possible for the older wooden boats to race competitively with those made from GRP. For example, the new hull, while being smooth, would have lines that were – 'a mean of the two older classes' and the existing sail plan would be maintained.

The job of building the new boats was given to Thames Structural Plastics of Canvey Island who charged £562 each for them. The new class was named the Estuary One-Design, with a red triangle as its sail insignia. After a slow start, with only three Estuary ODs racing with thirteen of the old boats during the first season, the class gained in popularity and an Association was formed in 1977 which absorbed the old Essex One-Design Association in 1988.

The last E.O.D. to be built was *Dafila*, for which Peter Wilson of Aldeburgh had to charge Brian Watling £9,000 in 1986.

In 1981, Aiden Boyack donated his E.O.D. *Arabesque* to the National Maritime Museum at Greenwich.

Regensboog (Rainbow) Class

Length Overall: 26ft 3in (8m)
Length Waterline: 17ft (5.2m)
Beam: 6ft 5in (1.9m)
Draught: 3ft 7in (1m)
Sail Area: 390 sq ft (35 sq m)
Designer: De Vries Lentsch
Builders: Various

It is surprising that this famous Dutch one-design class was introduced during World War One, the first boat being launched in 1917. The idea behind it came from a Congress of Watersport at which it was decided that there was a need in the Netherlands for a keel-boat that would cost less to build and maintain than the various metre classes that were popular only with those who could afford them.

A design submitted by the renowned yard of de Vries Lentsch was accepted. It was for a 26ft carvel-built boat, rather like the Broads OD, with a ballasted fin keel. It was optimistically hoped that the price could be kept down to 732 guilders, but it turned out that the first batch of boats cost around 1700 guilders each.

There was some delay before the first boat was built because orders for twenty boats were placed and de Vries Lentsch had to extend their building space in order to produce that number of hulls. It was while the first four boats were standing unfinished in the shed that a decision was made to have each one painted a different colour – hence the name Rainbow. But eventually, with more than a hundred boats in the Class, this proved to be a difficult rule to observe, and it was

dropped. The Rainbows have always been built in wood, although the types of timber used have varied according to availability throughout two World Wars and the years between. Recently the West™ epoxy system of construction has been used for new boats as well as for the rebuilding of some of the older ones.

The rig of a Rainbow has remained the same since its inception – a high peaked gaff mainsail with a slightly curved gaff and a solid wood mast in a tabernacle (again like the Brown Boats of the Broads) and supported by a forestay, a single pair of shrouds and a pair of running backstays. The area of the mainsail is 300 square feet, with another 90 square feet allowed for the No.1 jib. A spinnaker of 130 square feet is also permitted. The Rainbows are normally sailed with a crew of three and there is much hiking out for the two forward hands. Between the Wars some ninety Rainbows were built, but after 1945 interest in the Class waned until a meeting of owners was called and a Class association was formed, with links to the Royal Netherlands Sailing and Rowing Club.

In the early days of the Class, many owners of Rainbows were members of the Sailing

This Dutch boat was designed by De Vries Lentsch during the First World War and many of them are still racing keenly.

and Rowing Club of Muiden, but later, a strong fleet was also established in Friesland and annual team races are still held at Alkmaar between the Hollanders and the Frieslanders.

By the time the 75th Jubilee year of the Class had been reached in 1992, 134 boats had been built and No 1 was still sailing.

A couple of Rainbows in Friesland. Their rig has not changed since 1917 and the Class rules allow no such mechanical aids as sheet winches. Photo: Peter Chesworth

Shannon One-Design

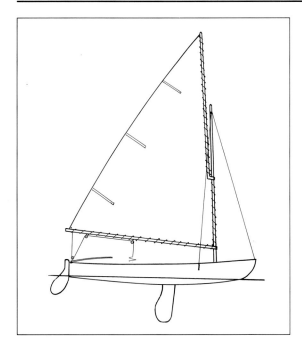

Length Overall: 18ft (5.5m)
Length Waterline: 17ft (5.2m)
Beam: 4ft 9in (1.4m)
Draught: 8in (0.2m)
Sail Area: 140 sq ft (13 sq m)
Designer: Morgan Giles
Builder: W Levinge

Morgan Giles must have been a very busy man during the years just after World War I, because he was called upon to design a number of different clench-built open or half-decked centreboard dinghies for clubs as widespread as Leigh-on-Sea in Essex, Dartmouth in Devon and Lough Ree in the middle of Ireland.

The Shannon One-Design Class, inevitably known as the SODs, came into being in the 1800s, as an alternative to the 'Lake' boats; centreboarders that had been popular during the latter part of the 1890s and the first two decades of this century. The Lake boats had been used for picnicking, fishing, rowing and for sailing, and these pastimes were expected to be possible with the new design.

Morgan Giles was approached and in 1921 he came up with plans for an 18ft open dinghy with a beam of 4ft 9in and a centreplate weighing 112lbs. The first boat was built locally by Walter Levinge, who charged £37-00 for her. Formal rules for the Class were established in 1926 and one of the first changes thereafter was to halve the weight of the centreboard. Then, in 1961, after Uffa Fox had likened the original lugsail rig as being – 'as antiquated as the banner under which King Billy crossed the Boyne', Morgan Giles was approached for a more modern sail plan. At first he was adamant that a 'one-design is intended to stay as such', but subsequently agreed to produce a new plan, using Terylene in place of cotton. But the spars remained and still are wooden. The boats, most of which were built by Walter Levinge, are planked in either spruce or elm with grown oak stem, sternpost, breast hook and knees.

The Shannon OD is usually raced with a crew of three, two of whom help mainly by bailing and sitting out, since there is no headsail to tend. The main fleets are on Lough Ree and Lough Derg and each season regattas are held during successive weeks at the two venues. Results of both weeks are combined to find the champion.

Gaviotta, S.O.D. No 46, seen here in the 1950s.
Photo: J.O. Simmons

The Shannon OD *Kiwi*, built in 1922, seen here sailing on Lough Ree in 1990.
Photo Gerry Murray

Between the Wars

The First World War put a stop to almost all pleasure sailing in Britain, and it was not until 1921 that the first post-war one-design class appeared in the UK. Once again Alfred Westmacott was the designer and he was asked for a boat to replace the original Mermaid that had been designed by G.V. Laws back in 1907, the old boats having been sold to the Medway Yacht Club and renamed the Jewell Class.

The new class of Mermaids, (which were destined to be replaced again in 1960 by GRP boats) were 24ft 6in overall, with a beam of 6ft and a draught of 3ft 5in. It seems that Westmacott, who was in charge of Woodnutts the builders, wanted the Seaview Yacht Club to allow him to sell the new boats to anyone, but permission was refused. Furthermore, the club, against the advice of the designer, required changes to be made, the effect of which made them difficult to handle in heavy weather. So next year Westmacott must have been pleased to be asked by Capt. Basil Lubbock of the Hamble River Sailing Club to design an 'improved' Mermaid.

The Sunbeam Class

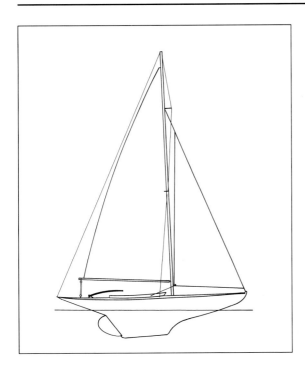

Length Overall: 26ft 5in (8m)
Length Waterline: 17ft 6in (5.3m)
Beam: 6ft (1.8m)
Draught: 3ft 9in (1.1m)
Sail Area: 300 sq ft (28 sq m)
Designer: A Westmacott
Builders: Various

The new class was to be named the Sunbeam and the boats were two feet longer and drew four inches more than the Seaview Mermaids, although they had the same beam. The Sunbeam carries 50 square feet of sail more than the Mermaid and although Westmacott gave them a firmer bilge the first boats proved to be rather tender and it was decided to add first 150 lbs and then a further 100 lbs of internal ballast. The necessary lead pigs were cast to fit between floors and shaped to the hull to prevent shifting in a seaway. Woodnutts of St. Helens, on the Isle of Wight, built 39 boats before the outbreak of war in 1939 and they were all given names ending in 'Y'.

Because the letter 'V' was chosen as the sail insignia for the Sunbeam Class, they are sometimes mistakenly thought to be members of the Victory Class, which is identified by the letter 'Z'.

In 1924, the Solent Sunbeams attracted the attention of the Royal Cornwall Yacht Club, who ordered eight boats from Woodnutts before forming the Falmouth Sunbeam Division. For the first few years the Solent Sunbeams raced from the Hamble River and rather strangely, their numbers were limited by a class rule to 24 boats so that two boats built at Itchenor were barred from racing with the class. Capt. Lubbock, who had introduced the Class, retired as Captain and the fleet transferred to Bembridge, where it remained until the outbreak of war in 1939. After the War, the restriction in numbers was removed and Sir Geoffrey Lowles and H.J.Ellam re-established the Class at Itchenor, where it has since remained.

The rules governing the two Sunbeam Divisions differ in certain respects; for instance, the Solent boats still carry 250lbs of internal ballast whereas the Falmouth fleet may carry up to 450 lbs. While the Solent boats are allowed spinnakers, those at Falmouth must be content with boomed out headsails, for which purpose they devised a special arrangement they call 'kitty gear'.

In recent years there have sometimes been more Sunbeams racing at Falmouth than in Chichester Harbour, but the two fleets, usually numbering more than twenty boats, compete together during Cowes Week when the multi-coloured hulls of what many people consider Alfred Westmacott's prettiest design, always make a grand show.

Although not intended for cruising, Sunbeams have occasionally made quite long passages in the open sea. One particular boat – *Danny* (V26), having been barred from the Solent fleet, migrated to Jersey in 1948. Owned by the two brothers John and Frank Breakwell, she left Itchenor on Sunday May 16th with four rolls in the main and when approaching the Island many hours later, they were hit by a gale which they rode out with a sea anchor streamed astern. *Danny* was driven off course towards Guernsey, but when the storm abated the brothers got under-way again with nine rolls in the main and reached Jersey on Thursday May 20th. After spending fifteen years in Jersey, *Danny* joined the Falmouth fleet, sailing the 130 miles to the Fal in thirty five hours.

The Sunbeam *Fay* (V24) racing during Cowes Week 1992. Photo: Yacht Shots

Dainty, the first Solent Sunbeam, was designed by Alfred Westmacott and built by
Woodnutt & Co. on the Isle of Wight in 1923. Photo: Christel Clear

St. Mawes One-Design

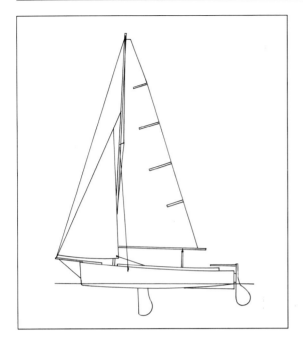

Length Overall: 16ft (4.9m)
Length Waterline: 15ft 10in (4.8m)
Beam: 6ft 1in (1.8m)
Draught: 10ins (4ft) – (0.3m &
1.2m)
Sail Area: 180 sq ft (16.5 sq m)
Designer: Frank Peters

There had been a one-design class at St Mawes in Cornwall before the one that sails there now. That was in the early nineteen twenties but only four boats were built to a design by Mr. Frank Green.

Frank Peters, a boat builder on the Percuil River, was a very keen sailor and in 1923 he produced a 16-foot, carvel-planked, gunter-rigged boat named *Aileen*, after his wife. The new boat, a centreboarder with a cast-iron plate and internal ballast, was very successful. Although building them was something of a sideline for Peters, others were ordered to the same design and that was how the present St. Mawes One-Design Class came into being. At the rate of about two each year, Peters had built fourteen of the boats before World War II. In 1938, permission was given to the Ponsharden Boat Yard to build seven boats to the Peters design for the Royal Cornwall Yacht Club. After the War Peters built a further six boats and by the 1960s sail numbers had reached 34.

In 1953, the owner of *Rainbow* (No. 23), improved the jaws of his mainsail gaff to get it closer to the mast. This alteration improved the boat's windward performance and at the same time caused quite a stir among other members of the class, which decided the time had come to change the rules to allow a taller mast and Bermudan rig.

As happened with other one-design classes, there followed a period of decline in popularity when increasing costs prevented new building. Then, in 1980 a Class Association was formed for the first time and after that the Class took on a new lease of life, with two new boats being built as recently as 1989.

The St Mawes Town Regatta Cup Race is regarded as the most important event for the St. Mawes ODs and usually attracts between 10 and 15 entries. In 1992, the ninetieth anniversary of Frank Peters, Commodore of the Class, was celebrated by a race that attracted 14 boats and was won by *Curlew* (No. 5), built by Frank in 1927.

Persephone was built by the Ponsharden Boat Yard in 1937 and would have been gunter-rigged when first launched. Photo: Lean Vercoe

A half dozen St. Mawes ODs just after the start of a race in 1980. Photo: Douglas Barton.

Gareloch One-Design

Length Overall: 24ft (7.3m)
Length Waterline: 16ft 6in (5m)
Beam: 5ft 6in (1.7m)
Draught: 3ft 9in (1.1m)
Sail Area: 224 sq ft (20 sq m)
Designer: McGruer & Co
Builder: McGruer & Co

The story of the Gareloch One-Design Class demonstrates once again just how much the fortunes of a class almost always depend upon the efforts of one or two dedicated people.

In the case of the Gareloch ODs, that person was John Henderson whose father owned *Iris*, one of the first batch to be built, while his son owns her now.

John Henderson has told the story up to 1959 in a history of the Class entitled 'Gareloch Goddesses'.

The Gareloch Yacht Club was formed just after the First World War and within a few years some members, like those of so many other clubs at that time, decided that they needed a one-design class. A committee of prospective owners asked McGruer & Co of Clynder to produce a design for a small boat of about 3 tons Thames Measurement, which was a common way of broadly describing a boat in those days.

A beautiful looking 24-footer was the result and a batch of ten of them was built in 1924 at a cost of £160 each.

The hulls were planked with half-inch pine on American elm timbers. The spars were and still are solid spruce and the rig was and still is Bermudan, although the booms were subsequently shortened as with so many other classes.

Lots were drawn by the intended owners before the first ten hulls were painted, and all the boats were named after Greek Goddesses.

The Gareloch ODs were originally three-quarter decked, but later some owners added removable cabin tops and more recently permanent cuddys have been added, rather like the Dragons.

While the first boats were being built, several members of the Royal Forth Yacht Club visited Clynder and were so impressed by them that they too ordered five boats for sailing on the Forth. McGruers managed to build them within six weeks so that they were racing by July of that same year.

The ten boats on the Gareloch raced happily against each other with little difference between their performance, until the coming of the Dragons to the Clyde in 1935. After that support for the Class declined and the Gareloch Yacht Club was wound up in 1936. The Class continued to race on the Forth, but there again interest declined when the Dragons came to Granton. Then, towards the end of the 1930s, some members of the Aldeburgh Yacht Club in Suffolk bought five Gareloch ODs from the Forth and two others from the Clyde.

After World War II, three small fleets of Gareloch ODs were sailing on the Clyde, the

The Gareloch OD fleet seen against a background of Argyll hills. Photo: Gordon Mucklow

The Gareloch OD, *Athene,* when she was painted yellow; followed by *Juno,* (No. 12)
Photo: Gordon Mucklow

Forth and the River Alde.

But it was not long before the Dragons came to Aldeburgh and once again the popularity of the smaller boat declined. So, when it was learned that John Henderson was trying to get all the Garelochs back to the Clyde, the Aldeburgh Yacht Club sportingly agreed to sell all of them, except *Iris*, back to their birthplace.

From that time the Class was effectively reborn and several of the new owners were helmsmen and helmswomen of the younger generation – exactly what is required if any class is to survive.

By 1956, eleven of the original sixteen boats were back on the Clyde and John Henderson envisaged the possibility of eventually getting all of them back where they had started. This meant recovering boats from places as far apart as the Forth, Aldeburgh and Bucklers Hard on the Solent. By 1957, fifteen boats were back and finally in August of that year *Iris* came back from Aldeburgh to fulfil John Henderson's dream.

West Wight Scow

Length Overall: 11ft 3in (3.42m)
Length Waterline: 10ft (3m)
Beam: 4ft 9in (1.4m)
Draught: 8in (3ft) – (0.2m & 0.9m)
Displacement: 210 lbs (95kg)
Sail Area: 65 sq ft (6 sq m)
Designer: B Hayward and T Smith
Builders: Various
Portsmouth Yardstick: 156

After the First World War, there was an interest in finding ways of encouraging children to learn to sail and with that aim in mind, in 1922, the Berthon Boat Company of Lymington produced what 'Yachting Monthly' described as 'a cheap and serviceable little knockabout boat'.

A number of similar boats had been built at Lymington before the War by George Courtney and Company, but Berthon set out not only to build complete boats, but for the first time also offer kits of parts for people to assemble at home. This idea was to become extremely popular when hardchine boats made from marine grade plywood became available after the Second World War, but perhaps because a fair amount of skill is required to build even a small lapstrake dinghy, Berthon sold more completed boats than kits of parts.

Several Lymington scows, as they came to be called, found their way across the Solent to Yarmouth where two keen dinghy sailors Herbert Reynolds and Dr Drummond, figured that they could improve on the Berthon design. So they approached Theo Smith, a local boatbuilder and in 1924, three new scows were launched at Yarmouth and the West Wight

Scow was born. The West Wight Scow Association was formed in 1926 and after 1925, scows were also built by Williams and Son in their yard at Cowes, so that by 1948 there were some 20 scows sailing at Yarmouth.

The West Wight Scow is 11ft 3in overall, has a beam of 4ft 9in and a galvanised steel centreplate that is adjusted by means of a notched lifting arm. Most scows were planked in spruce, and although they have a small foredeck there is no side decking. The West Wight version has only a single thwart, any crew having to sit on the bottom boards for much of the time without even the satisfaction of tending a foresail, since the 65 sq ft of sail area is all in a single standing lug.

During the 1920s and 30s., the idea of using scows to introduce youngsters to sailing and to amuse others who were not so young, caught on and before long there were fleets of these little clench-built dinghies on the River Hamble and at Portsmouth. The boats, although similar to the West Wight design, differed by a few inches here and there and sail area differed slightly. By the 1930s, there were 22 scows at Yarmouth, 18 on the Hamble, 30 at Lymington and some at Beaulieu, Keyhaven, Christchurch and even

Melanie Titmus and Lizzie Janes sailing Scow No. 404 during Otter Week at Burnham-on-Crouch in 1989. Photo: Coloryan

at Burnham-on-Crouch in Essex.

Although intended for beginners, the Solent Scows became popular with many experienced yachtsmen and women. Susan Hiscock, who had already sailed round the world with her husband Eric in the famous *Wanderer*, came back to Yarmouth in 1989 and began to sail a West Wight scow again after sixty years. Susan had always wanted to attend the annual meet of the Royal Cruising Club in her own boat, so in 1990 she sailed her scow *Shrimp* across the Solent to Beaulieu. The story was told in 'Yachting Monthly :-

"I sailed Shrimp *through Yarmouth's opening bridge at noon and set out with a fair southwesterly Force 3 to 4, keeping to the island shore because the tide was still foul. By the time I reached Hamstead Ledge, the ebb had finished and from there I headed direct for Beaulieu's entrance. It was a*

dead run and, as we rolled along with the lug sail squared off to port, I wondered how wise I was to run seven miles downwind. The lovely day encouraged me and there were dozens of yachts out enjoying the warmth and sunshine.

As usual, the wind was fresher off the entrance to Beaulieu where I gybed and brought the wind on the beam to tear into the river. There were two large motor-cruisers, apparently racing each other out over the bar, and in that shallow water their combined wash looked roughish and was in fact the only water I shipped during the passage.

Passing the Coastguard cottages on the first bend, I was in smooth water and tacked up towards the fleet, excited to be amongst some famous yachts and I wondered how many I would recognise. Someone hailed, 'Hello Susan' and I was invited aboard

Callisto Mio, *a Rustler 31 for a cup of hot coffee. I decided against staying on for the evening party, as I did not want to cross the Solent in the dark. There was also the possibility that the wind might go down with the sun. I did not want to row home.*

Before leaving the river, I moored to a post and put on my oilskins. Then I ran for the entrance, venturing across the flats to cut off the corner, the tide being higher and rising. Outside I brought Shrimp *on the wind to do her best with the flood, which soaked us away unmercifully to the East. We managed to fetch into Gurnard Bay and tried working along the shore in short tacks; there was no progress against the wind and tide, so I anchored. My fat little scow, though a delight to sail in smooth water, gets knocked back in a small chop; punch, punch, wallop; then start again, ad nauseam.*

I got out my sandwiches and watched with some irritation the effortless way a couple of sailboards swooped around, oblivious of the tide. Sitting on the floorboards and leaning against the middle (and only) thwart, I thought of a nap as I was going to be late home. Have you tried a nap in similar circumstances? It's roll, roll, jump and bang-bang from the heavy metal centreboard, plus the enchanting chuckle as only a clinker-built boat knows how. The sun set before eight and the moon climbed over the island. By the time I had Saltmead Ledge buoy abeam, it was quite dark, the ebb was with me and the wind holding. I dismissed all thoughts of entering Newtown. It might have been difficult to see my way in. Quickly we whisked past Hamstead Ledge, passing seaward of the buoy to avoid the rough water and barrage between it and the shore. Then only Yarmouth lay ahead with the moon illuminating the numerous obstacles. Rounding the pier, the harbour's FULL notice was up and I needed an oar to help me through the crowd of yachts. It was midnight when I stepped ashore; a good day with the night passage a spicy bonus."

Susan Hiscock sailing *Shrimp,* her West Wight Scow. Photo: Jennifer Nicholls

Hamble River Star Class

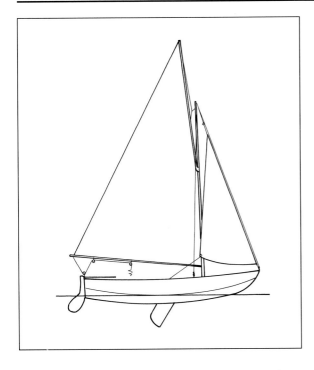

Length Overall: 14ft (4.3m)
Length Waterline: 11ft 6in (3.5m)
Beam: 5ft (1.5m)
Draught: 9in (2ft 9in) – (0.2m & 0.8m)
Sail Area: 110 sq ft (10 sq m)
Designer: A.R. Luke
Builder: Luke Bros.

In 1925 A. R. Luke of Luke Brothers on the Hamble designed a simple 14ft open dinghy that was rather unusual in that it has a semi hard-chine hull. The boats were planked in mahogany and spruce and while the topsides are curved, they are 'V' shaped below the waterline.

The boats are gunter-rigged, with a small jib taking only 20 of the 120 sq ft total sail area.

At first Hamble Stars were sailed locally by The Hamble River SC and the Household Brigade YC. Later, a fleet of ten boats was established at the Thorney Island SC in Chichester Harbour. After World War II, the remainder of the South Coast fleets migrated to the Thames, where the Erith YC still race and use them for instruction.

Sail insignia is a five-pointed star above the class number of the boat.

A couple of Hamble River Stars sailing on the Thames at Erith after their transfer from the Hamble.

'Fife' 16ft One-Design Class

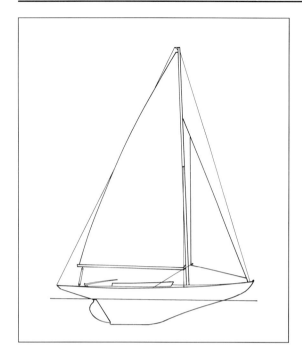

Length Overall: 24ft 4in (7.4m)
Length Waterline: 16ft (4.9m)
Beam: 6ft 4in (1.9m)
Draught: 3ft 3in (1m)
Sail Area: 250 sq ft (23 sq m)
Designer: William Fife
Builder: Dickie & Sons

The Conway and Menai Straits One-Design Class, as it was called in 1926, when William Fife designed and Dickie and Sons built the first of these 24ft Bermudan sloops; now sail under the auspices of the Royal Anglesey Yacht Club at Beaumaris.

In 1940, 'Yachting World' claimed that these 16ft Fife boats were 'generally regarded as being the thoroughbreds of the racing fleet'. Certainly they are handsome boats; not unlike a small Dragon but with shorter overhangs.

In the early 1920s, the Conway Yacht Club was still racing in Conway Restricted Class boats, which operated under a length and sail area rule requiring that after adding the load water-line length to the square root of the sail area and then halving it, the result had to be 15. This rule proved unsatisfactory and led one authority to proclaim that it 'encouraged winners of a most undesirable type.'

So some members of the Club decided to make a fresh start by asking William Fife for a design that would combine a waterline length of 16ft with a modest draught of 3ft 3in and produce a boat that would provide good racing as well as day sailing and 'small' cruising. Draught was restricted to just over three feet because of the 'depth of water

conveniently available in the Conway and Menai Straits.'

The first boat, *Sian II* was built in the winter of 1926/27 and cost £275 complete. As happened with several other classes there was no Number 3 boat because of the likelihood of confusing sails bearing 3 or 8 when seen from a distance. Between 1926 and 1938, Dickie built fifteen wooden boats for the Class, most of which are still racing. The hulls were relatively lightly constructed, being planked with Honduras mahogany and decked with laid pine.

The rig was Bermudan from the outset; with running backstays until the boom was shortened and the mast lengthened in 1950 to allow the use of a standing backstay, and so reduce the risk of broken masts.

After the War, Uffa Fox took an interest in the Class, having sailed in *Siglen* (No 7), whose rig he modified by removing the topmast forestay and adding jumper struts – in the style of the Dragon. Again, as with the Dragons, metal masts were allowed for the Fife 16s in the 1960s and since then most, but not all of the boats have alloy spars.

No new wooden boats were built after the War and the Class would have probably gone into decline if the Association had not decided to allow Fife 16s to be built in GRP. The decision was made in the early 1970s and a mould was obtained from the hull of *Merlin*, one of the last of the wooden boats to have been built before the War. To equalise displacement, it was found necessary to add 1 cwt. to the ballast keels of the GRP hulls. Dickies of Bangor continued to be the sole builder and the first GRP boat *Fleur* (No 20), was launched in 1972. Since then 23 other glass fibre hulls have been produced, the most recent one in 1979.

The GRP boats race against the older wooden boats and as with the Dragons, an old boat sometimes wins. In any case there are still some trophies reserved for the wooden boats . One of these is the Charles Livingstone Trophy, presented by the original owner of *Sian II* (No 1), and recently restored by his son David.

Sian II, was the first of the Conway and Menai Straits 'Fife' ODs to be built. Although Bermudan-rigged from the beginning, the sail plan of the Class was 'modernized' in 1950. Photo: John Brooke

Photo overleaf:
These 'Fifes are all GRP boats. Their hulls were laid up on a mould that was made by using the hull of *Merlin*. Photo: William Rowntree

Brightlingsea One-Design

Length Overall: 18ft (5.5m)
Length Waterline: 17ft 3in (5m)
Beam: 6ft 1in (1.8m)
Draught: 10in (5ft) (0.25m & 1.5m)
Sail Area: 220 sq ft (20 sq m)
Designer: Robert Stone
Builders: Various
Portsmouth Yardstick: 115

After the First World War, yacht racing at Brightlingsea, on the river Colne in Essex, was organised mainly in two handicap classes for boats that were either under or over 21 feet. This was typical of the position many clubs were in until it was remedied by the introduction of local one-design classes. In 1927 a local designer – Robert ('Robbie') Stone presented a set of plans to the Brightlingsea Sailing Club for an 18-foot clench-built, three-quarter-decked centreboard boat. The club accepted the design and the Brightlingsea One-Design Class was born. The first three boats were built by D. Stone & Sons and were sailing in 1928.

Stone's design was very much like the Thames Estuary OD that had been sailing off the Southend shore since 1911. The dimensions of the two boats were the same within an inch or so and in due course, when the numbers of T.E.O.D.s had declined, they often raced on level terms against the Brightlingsea boats during Burnham Week.

Unlike the original T.O.D., but like the Essex OD, the Brightlingsea boats were Bermudan rigged from the start and both these classes originally had short bowsprits. A revised rig was designed for the B.O.Ds

by Robert Stone in 1951 and one boat, *White Magic* used the new sail plan, which did not require a bowsprit.

There followed several years of dispute about the new rig and things became so heated at one point that it was ruled that the matter would not be discussed again during a period of three years. During that time, those boats that had adopted the new rig were required to sail as a separate section of the Class. But by 1957, most of the fleet had modernised their rigs and the whole of the Class raced together again.

Until 1957 all Brightlingsea ODs had been built by D. Stone & Sons or James & Stone – the company that absorbed the original builder. At that point the Class Association decided that because neither of the previous builders held title to Robert Stone's design, the Association was free to have a new set of drawings made from an existing boat and then have moulds made that would become the property of the Association.

Since then a number of different yards have built to the design, the most recent being Malcolm Goodwin of Wivenhoe, who completed *Avocet* in 1991.

A line of Brightlingsea ODs racing in the Colne during the Colne Week Regatta in 1951. Note the bowsprits. Photo: F. Armes

The Brightlingsea OD, *Viking*, ahead of a couple of Estuary ODs during a Burnham Week race in 1990, when they competed as one Class. Photo: Coloryan.

Troy One-Design

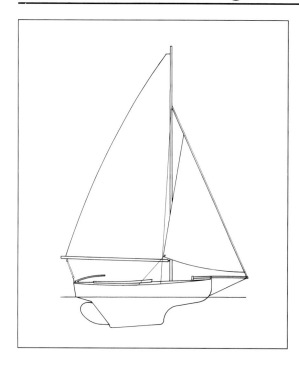

T

Length Overall: 18ft (5.5m)
Length Waterline: 17ft 6in (5.3m)
Beam: 6ft (1.8m)
Draught: 3ft 9in (1.1m)
Sail Area: 298 sq ft (27 sq m)
Designer: A.H.Watty
Builder: A.H.Watty

Even though only twenty one boats were ever built to the design, I am including the Troy Class.

The first of the boats that came to be known as the Troys, was designed and built by Archie Watty of Fowey in 1928 at the request of Sir Charles Hanson. She was called *Joselyn* and while she was being built, a local bank manager, Mr Strong, took a liking to her and ordered another, which he named *Anemone*. After that, Watty obtained orders for two further boats and took a chance on building two more on spec. By 1930 there were six boats afloat, so their owners decided to form an Association and having obtained the approval of Sir Arthur Quiller-Couch, they called them the 'Troys'.

The 21st Troy One-Design, called *Brilliant*, was built in 1990 by Maurice Hunkin at Bodinnick-by-Fowey on the eastern shore of the river. The joint owners of the new boat were Terry Vernon and Ed Dubois, both of whom were probably better known in connection with ORC and IOR events. Ten years had elapsed since T20 *Maid of*

Polruan had been built by John Fuge, a Watty apprentice, who reckoned that a new set of moulds should be used to build *Brilliant*.

Archie Watty died in 1949, and although several more Troys were built in the yard, it was finally closed in 1970. After that the Class Association bought the moulds and made it known that any local builder could use them for a small fee.

The Troy is a strongly-built 'no-nonsense' kind of boat, carvel-planked and 18 feet overall with a straight stem and an almost vertical transom stern. She has a beam of 5ft 9in and a draught of 3ft 9in with a longish 16 cwt lead ballast keel. Originally the Troys were gaff-rigged with a jib set on a bowsprit and a total area of about 260 square feet. Then much more quickly than happened with most other classes, it was decided in 1934 to switch to a Bermudan rig, which meant a longer mast and a shorter boom. Later a further change was made to allow a larger headsail, a total sail area of 300 square feet and the use of a spinnaker.

A group of Troy ODs with a couple of intruders, seen in Falmouth Harbour in 1950. The Troys are: *Jocelyn* (T1), *Anenome* (T2), *Shimmer* (T4), *Sapphire* (T7) and *Aquamarine* (T16). Photo: Graham Gullick.

Ruby (T6), built in 1932, was sailed with great success by Mr. W.H. Graham and then by his son Michael. Photo: Marcus Lewis.

Conway One-Design

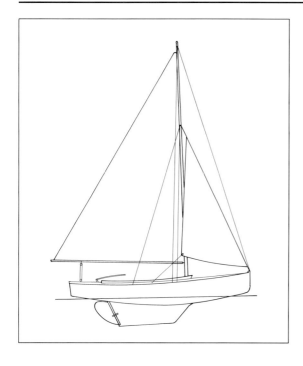

Length Overall: 20ft (6.1m)
Length Waterline: 15ft 10in (4.8m)
Beam: 6ft 7in (2m)
Draught: 3ft (0.9m)
Sail Area: 212 sq ft (19.5 sq m)
Designer: W.H. Rowland
Builders: Various

In 1928, the same year that saw the first Troy OD, another new one-design class was established by the Conway Yacht Club on the Menai Strait. Unlike the Troy, the Conway boat was the result of a positive decision of the Club to establish a class to replace the Conway and Menai Strait Fife One-Design boats they had been sailing. The 'Fife' One-Design, as it had come to be called because of its famous designer, is a fair-sized Bermudan sloop; 24ft 6in overall with moderate overhangs, a beam of 6ft 4in and drawing only a fraction over 3 feet. When carrying the permitted 256 square feet of sail it was perhaps not surprising that some considered the Fife boats rather tender.

In profile the new and smaller Conway One-Design is rather like the Troy, with a straight stem and almost vertical transom. But there the similarity ends, because the Conway boat has a flat bilge and a fin keel. The original design was by a member of the Club, W.H. Rowland, and the first boat, a centreboarder was built for Norman Jones by Matthew Owen at Menai Bridge in 1928. *Seiriol* as she was called, sailed as a centreboarder in the handicap class during her first season and proved to be virtually

unbeatable. However, by the time it had been decided to establish a new class the decision was also made to replace the centreplate with a fin keel supporting 6 cwt of outside ballast. A keel was also added to *Seiriol* and she was still sailing in the class in 1990.

The Conway OD is a three quarter-decked carvel-planked 20 footer with 6ft 7in beam and 3ft draught. The first four keel boats were built by the designer of the Class and the next two by Dickie of Bangor. After that, in 1935, three more boats were built by Rileys of Deganwy, home of the Conway Yacht Club. These three boats had a hollower sheer than those built earlier and they became known as the 'banana' boats. Before the War, Dickies built another ten boats, while Leavett of Beaumaris built a further pair.

From the outset, the Conway OD, was Bermudan-rigged, with a low aspect mainsail of 167 square feet and a foresail of 46 square feet. A spinnaker can be set inside the forestay.

As with all one-designs that began as wooden boats, the inevitable arguments constantly arose about the wisdom of accepting GRP construction for the Conway OD. By the late 1980s, most of the members of the Conway Yacht Club believed that the only way to keep the Class alive was to make new construction cheaper and this meant building in GRP. The acceptance of GRP construction means that a plug must be made, but before that can be done a compromise must also be agreed in order to reconcile any differences that exist between wooden boats that are already in the class.

After the members of the Club had decided to pay for a plug, they approached the Ferry Boatyard in Penketh, where Eric Bergquist agreed to take on the project. He enlisted the aid of Peter Farrer, an engineer and together they set out to produce a GRP hull that would be neither faster nor slower than the wooden boats and would retain those characteristics of the wooden hulls that had appealed to members for half a century. For instance the slight tumble home in the after sections and the hollow sheer of the 'banana' boats.

The first GRP boat was ordered by Pam MacDonald, who named her *Phoenix* and to everyone's relief, rigged with a mast and sails from an older boat. The new recruit sailed in the middle of the fleet most of the time but occasionally won.

Acushla (No.11) and *Kathleen* (No. 6), two wooden Conway ODs, racing off Beaumaris during the Menai Straits Fortnight in 1985. Photo: William Rowntree.

International Dragon

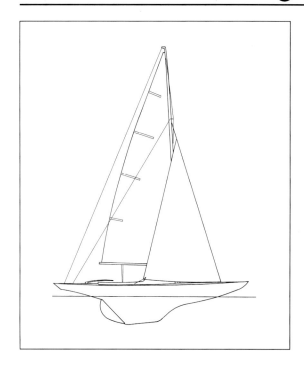

D

Length Overall: 29ft (8.9m)
Length Waterline: 18ft 6in (5.65m)
Beam: 6ft 4in (1.95m)
Draught: 3ft 11in (1.20m)
Displacement: 3747lbs (1700kg)
Sail area: 290 sq ft (27 sq m)
Designer: J. Anker
Builders: Various
Portsmouth Yardstick:107

The International Dragon is particularly interesting because without ever being intended as a one-design boat, it has become one of the most successful of international one-design classes, and was selected for seven Olympic Games between 1948 and 1972.

Uffa Fox was quick to see the potential of the Dragon when, in 1937 he wrote:-

"The Dragons have the qualities sought for in one-design classes. They will continue and prosper."

Uffa's foresight has been realised and by 1992, some 1,400 Dragons were registered with National Associations in twenty countries, while hundreds more were still being sailed, although not necessarily racing.

The Dragon was the result of a competition organised by the Royal Yacht Club of Gothenburg in 1929, for a small two-berth keel-boat that could be used for simple weekend cruising among the islands and fiords of the Scandinavian seaboard. The winning design was by Johan Anker of Norway, who was the designer and helmsman of the winning boat in the 12 metre class at the Olympic Games of 1912 and the lines of the Dragon are really those of a very small metre class boat. Johan Anker died in 1940, but not before

he had seen his creation become popular throughout Scandinavia and in the UK.

In 1946, W.M. Mackinlay, secretary of the Clyde Yacht Clubs' Conference, visited Norway and learned from Johan Anker's son Erik, that before he died, his father had insisted that in recognition of what British seamen had done for Norway during the War, no designer's royalty would ever be asked of any British owner or builder of a Dragon.

The Dragon is 8.9m overall, but only 5.65m on the waterline, with a beam of 1.95m, and a draught of 1.2m, and a cast-iron ballast keel weighing 1,000kg. Originally the boats had small cabins with two berths, but gradually the 'cabin' has been reduced to a mere cuddy and no doubt would have disappeared altogether but for a rule which requires the length of the 'cabin' top to be at least one metre.

The first Dragons had a sail area of 20 square metres and spinnakers were not allowed until 1938, but since then the combined area of the main and genoa has been increased to almost 27 square metres. The mast, which at that time was wooden, had one pair of long cross-trees and standing

Troika, built in 1961, one of the fleet of Dragons at the Royal Norfolk and Suffolk YC, seen racing off Lowestoft. Photo: Peter Hawes.

The first fleet of U.K. Dragons was established in Scotland in 1936. Here, some of them are seen racing on the Clyde soon after the War. Photo: Ian Gilchrist

fore and back stays from the masthead. In 1945 the topmast forestay was removed and diamond stays and jumper struts together with shorter cross-trees allowed a genoa to be properly sheeted and a spinnaker to be set around a single lower forestay.

When they introduced the Dragon, it was the purpose of the Royal Yacht Club of Gothenburg to have a cheap boat that young people could afford, and with this in mind the original specification required all boats to be planked with pine – a readily available wood in Scandinavia. This rule was replaced later, when boats came to be built all over the world and mahogany was sometimes cheaper than pine.

The way in which the Dragon came to Scotland and then to the rest of the UK, is interesting. In 1933, A.H. Ball, a member of the Royal Clyde YC was cruising in Scandinavia where he saw and was so impressed by the Dragon that he obtained a set of plans and brought them back to show

his fellow yachtsmen in Scotland. It so happened that the Clyde clubs were already looking for a small boat to replace the large and expensive pre-war classes.

Despite lack of interest from the Yacht Racing Association and objections from the old guard that they did not want – 'foreign designed and foreign built boats', J Howden-Hume and George Paisley announced that they had already bought a Dragon called *Anita* and she could be inspected in McGruer's yard at Clynder. The first six British Dragons were in fact built by McGruer who charged £220 apiece for them.

The success of the Class in Scotland was immediate, and by 1936 there were 14 Dragons sailing on the Clyde, where the first of a series of international races was held and the Clyde Yacht Clubs Conference presented the Dragon Gold Cup, which has remained the most coveted international trophy.

After the War, the Class was taken over in Britain by the RYA.

Kelpie, (ex *Pegasus*), caught in a squall off Roseneath Point in the Clyde.
Photo: Ian Gilchrist.

Unlike many other one-design classes, the rules do not specify the weight of a wooden Dragon, although they do require strict adherence to the specified scantlings together with the use of timbers having closely defined weights per cubic metre. Before 1973, most Dragons were carvel-planked in wood either caulked or close-seamed but many had glued planking – a technique much favoured by Borresen in Denmark before the acceptance of GRP construction in 1972.

The International Dragon Association, has had the foresight to modify the Class rules when necessary to permit for example, the use of synthetic sail cloth in 1957 and alloy spars in 1971.

When the first proposals were made to allow GRP construction, it was made clear that should the new hulls prove faster than those built of wood, then they would not be accepted into the Class. On the other hand if GRP hulls proved to be slower than those built from wood, there would be no problem because nobody would want them.

It was Borge Borresen, winner of the Gold Cup for Denmark on the Clyde in 1967 who, in collaboration with Lloyds Register of Shipping, produced the GRP specification that was accepted by the International Dragon Association in 1972. Since then most Dragons have been made with plastic hulls, although older wooden boats still manage to win the occasional open championship.

At first the rules required a boat to be built wholly of plastic, but later it became clear that many owners liked the idea of an easily maintained hull in combination with an attractive wooden deck and superstructure; and such composite construction is allowed, subject to prior approval of the IYRA. While the Star Class decided not to introduce a 'swing-test' to ensure that GRP hulls were not built with light ends, all GRP Dragons are required to undergo such a test to ensure that the lay-up was carried out according to specification.

Early in 1948, it was learned that Prince Philip, the Duke of Edinburgh, was looking for a second-hand Dragon because at that time building licences were only being granted for special purposes. On hearing this, members of the Island Sailing Club decided that since the Dragon had been chosen for the 1948 Olympics in Torbay, it would be appropriate to ask Princess Elizabeth and the Duke of Edinburgh to accept a Dragon Class yacht as a wedding gift. Some eyebrows were raised when it was announced that the new boat would be named *Bluebottle*, but there was no doubt that their Royal Highness's acceptance of the gift was greatly appreciated by small class yachtsmen everywhere. The Dragon was selected for six more Olympics after 1948, before being replaced by the Soling, after which many people felt that the Class would decline and die. That did not happen and there are other people who believe that the Class is better off out of the limelight and the extreme competition of those who campaign for gold medals.

Dragon sailors have plenty of trophies to compete for without Olympic medals. As early as 1937, the Clyde Yacht Club's Conference presented a Gold Cup for annual competition and this has remained the premier Dragon trophy. Then, in 1949 the Duke of Edinburgh presented the Edinburgh Cup for annual competition in British waters. Describing a race for the Gold Cup at Marstrand in 1958 when he was crewing for Aage Birch, Paul Elvstrom recalled :-

"I remember in the third race it was blowing like hell. Aage had not put on any fittings for a working jib and we said how can we possibly carry the genoa today. The wind speed was 21 metres per second (42 knots) during the race and all the other Dragons set their working jibs and when we were going out of the harbour I remember Ole Bernsten called out to us 'Oh no! that will not work this time'. But there was nothing else we could do so we went out.

We were starting on a dead run and we had the spinnaker pole on the genoa. It was blowing so hard that only one boat, sailed by Tokid Warrer, put up a spinnaker but immediately, 'bang', there were only three leeches left with no sail in between them.

We came to the lee mark first with a big group just behind and there was a lot of banging and crashing. We started up the beat and were looking at the mast and saw we had sheeted the mainsail too hard. So you took the mainsheet in your hand and only looked at the mast all the time. We pulled in the genoa and were sailing on the genoa and a tiny piece of the mainsail leech – just enough to keep the boat in balance. I think that was the day when we learnt that whatever happened you can keep a genoa up and it will always be better than a working jib.

We beat all the other Dragons so easily that day and afterwards no one put fittings on for working jibs any more. It showed that you shall never have another headsail than a genoa on a Dragon – never mind how much it blows."

A few old Dragons are still used for short cruises and for day sailing, but all newly built boats are intended for racing and although they are certainly seaworthy enough to sail in the open sea in almost any conditions, few of them could make the long voyages achieved by *Gerda* just after the War. Morin Scott has told the story graphically in his little book – 'Gerda's Sea Saga', and a few short extracts follow.

Photo Opposite:
Nortic, a wooden Borrensen boat built in 1972, is seen here racing during Cowes Week 1986. Photo: Janet Harber

Like most of the early Dragons, *Gerda* had a little cabin with a couple of berths and a primus stove, but as Scott says: – *"A Dragon's cabin is no place for humans in a lumpy sea particularly when one has to crouch over, and operate, one of Mr Simpson Lawrences's centrifuge pumps."*

After sailing *Gerda* from McGruer's yard on the Gareloch to Newhaven during the Spring of 1947, Scott and his crew, Conny van Rietschoten, heard that the International Gold Cup races were to be held in Norway in 1948 and they decided to sail across the North Sea to participate.

The voyage started from Woolverstone on the river Orwell in Suffolk – long before there was a marina there. By midnight they were out of Harwich Harbour and once clear of the Shipwash off Orfordness, course was changed to North 60° East after which they made six and a half knots for the rest of the night. By noon on the following day, conditions had deteriorated and –

". . . the little ship heeled over to a most alarming angle and remained there far too long to be healthy.

Much as it went against the grain to reduce her speed there was nothing for it but to lower the mainsail altogether... With the mainsail down and speed reduced to about five knots, she was much easier. Less water came aboard; she carried no helm and seemed to ride the waves more easily. In this way we drove on throughout the afternoon; Conny in the cabin pumping from time to time and myself at the tiller. Every hour or two we ate a tube of malted milk tablets.

Towards evening the wind abated slightly and at seven o'clock the mainsail was hoisted with seven rolls in it, and as the log showed that we had covered over a hundred miles since midnight, we began to keep an eye open for land ahead. Gerda made great speed and at 2130 lights were in sight ahead. These were identified as Den Helder, but, since it was now getting dark and the wind was increasing again, neither of us thought much of the idea of trying to navigate through the banks into the harbour. We then lowered the mainsail, gybed, and set off on a course on N, 20°E, determined to push on 'round the corner' at least.

Within an hour the Texel Light Vessel was sighted and having now definitely fixed our position life seemed much better. Wind and sea had increased through the night and by four o'clock in the morning the weather was about at its worst. We had been pooped several times (They had a canvas cover that kept some water out of the cockpit) and even when this was avoided water came aboard as we 'surf-rode' on the crests.

From inside the cabin Conny could see green water through the cabin ports on both sides at the same time! By this time I had been at the tiller for about nineteen hours and was not, understandably, one hundred per cent efficient. Conny was not any better off for he had been busily employed at the pump, chart, passing out the food etc. So it happened that at 0400, when my attention was caught by something else, we were pooped over the quarter again, but with more force than usual. The stern was flung round and the whole vessel literally thrown over onto her side and apparently held there by the pressure of the wind on mast, rigging and one sail, for what seemed like an eternity. The level of water (if anything was level in the ceaselessly heaving turmoil) was a third of the way up the cockpit cover. The cabin hatch was closed. I could feel the water pouring over the cockpit coaming, under the cover, onto my legs in considerable quantity. It seemed to go on for hours. Would she never come up?

At that moment I knew real fear. Then, after an age she came up and I could tell by her sluggish motion she was well nigh filled. As always after a big sea had come over, I shouted to Conny 'I'm here'. Then he shouted up: 'For God's sake sail her easy 'till I get this lot out or we've had it'. Believe you me, I sailed her carefully, and never have I heard such a welcome sound as that pump sucking dry."

More recently, Donald Street, best known for his book 'The Ocean Sailing Yacht' and his voyages in the venerable yawl *Iolaire*, sailed his 55-year-old Dragon *Gypsy* from the south coast of Ireland to Brest to take part in the classic boat celebrations held there in 1992.

Today's Dragon is a very different thing from the uncomplicated boat that Anker designed in 1929. Although electronics are barred (except for the use of echo-sounder by some fleets), rig and sail adjustments have become extremely complex, as the maze of control lines in the cockpit of any competitive Dragon will testify. There is also plenty of work for all three of the crew, particularly when the spinnaker is required. Strangely, in Norway, home of the Dragon, modernisation was resisted for many years and the Class went into decline. Happily, the Norwegian Dragon Association now accepts the international rules and aims, and their fleet is growing once again.

The author's Dragon *Cluaran*, was built by Roland in Norway in 1951.
Photo: Janet Harber

International 12 Square-Metre Sharpie

Length Overall: 19ft 8in (5.99m)
Length Waterline: 17ft 8in (5.4m)
Beam: 4ft 8in (1.43m)
Draught: 7in (3ft) – (0.16m & 0.96m)
Sail Area: 129 sq ft (12 sq m)
Designer: G. Kroger
Builders: Various

Like the Dragon, from which it could hardly be more different, the 12 square-metre Sharpie was the result of a design competition. In 1930, the Deutsche Segler Verband of Berlin were seeking – 'a two-man centreboard dinghy of high performance'. They probably had in mind a boat that would be suitable for the inland lakes around Berlin.

Gebruder Kroger won the competition with a design for a half-decked hard-chine boat that is almost 20 feet long but draws hardly more than 6 inches with the centreplate up. Within months the Sharpies were sailing in Germany and these were quickly followed by fleets in Holland and in England where, in 1932, the Ouse Amateur Sailing club ordered six boats from Kroger's yard in Germany.

Jan Sanderson, secretary of the British Sharpie Owners Association has described the arrival of the boats at Kings Lynn in Norfolk:-

"When finally the boats arrived they were lowered from the cargo ship still in their crates, into the dock. The proud new owners went alongside their Sharpies in rowing boats, hammered open the packing cases, stepped the masts, hoisted the sails, sailed the Sharpies out of the dock and immediately participated in a race on the River Ouse."

Twelve square-metre Sharpies have been sailing from clubs on the North Norfolk coast ever since.

Another batch of the German boats was imported that same year by the Barnt Green Sailing Club in Cheshire, while at Burnham-on-Crouch in Essex, the Royal Corinthian Yacht Club adopted the class in 1932, building nine boats for annual charter by their members. For some reason the first Burnham boats had Bermudan rather than gaff mainsails, but presumably still complied with a total sail area of 12 square metres.

After the war the Burnham fleet was enlarged when the class was adopted by the United Hospitals Sailing Club, so that by 1962, more than a dozen Sharpies competed for the Ariel Challenge Cup during Burnham Week.

A fleet of Sharpies was also established at Itchenor in Chichester Harbour and before the Second World War, there was team racing between the Royal Corinthian YC and Itchenor SC.

The 12 square-metre Sharpie is a heavily built boat, with sawn oak frames and 14mm mahogany planking assembled with the seam-batten form of construction. Overall length is 19ft 7in; waterline length approximately

The 12 Square-Metre Sharpie has always been popular in Holland, where more than seventy of them were still racing in 1992. These two are on the Braassemer Meer near Aalsmeer. Photo: Peter Chesworth.

Although the mast is still stepped in a tabernacle, a centre mainsheet tackle is often used in the Sharpie nowadays. Photo: Neil Foster.

17ft 8in; beam only 4ft 8in and draught 3ft with the plate down. It was meant to be a cheap boat and with that aim in mind, all metal fittings were made from steel and then galvanised. Most of the early boats were built at the famous yard of Abeking and Rasmussen at Lemwerder and in 1931, 'Yachting Monthly' carried an advertisement by the UK agent, offering complete boats for £40, although a certificate of racing did cost another 25 Shillings. Some Sharpies were even built in a field near Horsham in Sussex and were sold at £30 each, but they were poorly constructed and came to be known as the 'Horsham Coffins'.

Even though they were heavy, it was claimed that in a fresh breeze the 12 square-metre Sharpie was some 2-3 minutes per hour faster than a 14-foot International dinghy of those days – but that was before the 14s were allowed to use a trapeze.

In 1933, only a couple of years after its introduction, the International Yacht Racing Union accepted the 12 square-metre Sharpie as an International Class. After the War, the Class regained popularity so that in 1956 it was selected for the Olympic Games in Melbourne, where thirteen nations competed and the medals were won by New Zealand, Australia and the UK. That was the peak period for the 12 square-metre Sharpie and the Class was never again selected for the Olympics. Nevertheless, there are still small but lively fleets in the UK at Wells, Brancaster Staithe and Burnham Overy in Norfolk as well as at Langstone in Chichester Harbour. There are also active fleets in Holland, Germany, Portugal and Brazil. The 1991 European Sharpie Championship, held at Brancaster Staithe in Norfolk, attracted 54 entries and three of the competing boats were part of the batch that arrived at Kings Lynn in 1932. They were K8, K9 and K19 and all three finished the series among the top nine boats.

Several of these sixty-years-old boats, built by Abeking and Rasmussen, have been completely and lovingly rebuilt and now they certainly rank as 'classic one-designs'.

International Snipe Class

Length Overall: 15ft 6in (4.7m)
Length Waterline: 13ft 6in (4.1m)
Beam: 5ft (1.5m)
Draught: 6in (3ft 5in) – (0.15m & 1m)
Displacement: 381 lbs (172kg)
Sail Area: 112 sq ft (10 sq m)
Designer: W Crosby
Builders: Various

William Crosby was editor of 'The Rudder', the foremost American magazine for yachtsmen in the 1930s, when he had already gained a reputation as a designer. In 1931, a group of yachtsmen belonging to the Florida West Coast Racing Association asked Crosby to design a small boat that could be taken from place to place on a trailer. The only limits they set were that the boat should not be longer than 16ft and should not set more than 100 square feet of sail.

That was in March, and by July, 'The Rudder' published the lines, offsets, sailplan and construction details of a 15ft 6in, hard-chine dinghy with a galvanized iron dagger-plate. In accordance with its practice of naming designs after birds, 'The Rudder' called the new dinghy the Snipe, and to indicate that it was intended for trailing, the original sail insignia took the form of a motor car wheel and not the silhouette that subsequently came to be recognized throughout the world. The Snipe was an immediate success, largely because it could be built by unskilled amateurs. The hull was hard-chined – as the Star had been before – and the sawn frames remained in the boat. The deck was planked and canvas covered,

while the mast was a box-form construction without spreaders and the boom a simple 'T' section spar.

By November 1931, Crosby was able to write that – "This boat has proven to be one of the most popular designs of the entire Rudder series, dozens of them are being built by amateurs all over the world."

For a while, Crosby ran an unofficial class register from his office, issuing sail numbers free of charge.

Many of the early builders of Snipes had ideas for improving the original design and for a while Crosby used the pages of 'The Rudder' to broadcast these suggestions. But he soon realised that if Snipes were to race against each other on equal terms, a set of rules and specifications would have to be drawn up, accepted and observed. So he commissioned the building of a Snipe of his own, which did include some changes from the original, although the lines of the hull remained the same. The prototype was completed in the winter of 1931/2 after which a booklet was published containing photographs taken during construction of the boat and a copy was supplied with every set of plans.

Norfolk OD 14ft Dinghy

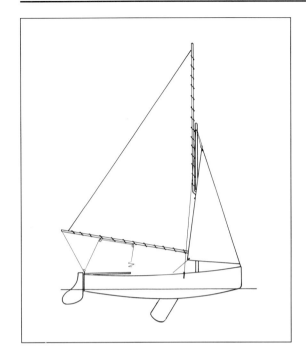

B

Length Overall: 14ft (4.3m)
Length Waterline: 13ft 3in (4m)
Beam: 5ft 41/2in (1.6m)
Draught: 7in (3ft 9in)
- (0.2m & 1.1m)
Sail Area: 132 sq ft (12 sq m)
Designer: Herbert Woods
Builder: Herbert Woods
Portsmouth Yardstick: 130

In the issue of the 'Eastern Daily Press" dated January 13th, 1931, there appeared a photograph of two fellows in a fourteen foot gunter rigged clench-built open dinghy being observed by its designer and builder, Herbert Woods of Potter Heigham in Norfolk. The text relating to the picture read:

"The much discussed £65 racing dinghy – a protest against those in the 14-ft International Class soaring to 150gns or more – is now an accomplished fact. The first of the new class has been built by Mr Herbert Woods of Potter Heigham, and in our illustration he is seen starting experts off on a trial trip. Mr W L Clabburn is at the helm and he is crewed by Mr C S Green. Previously Mr Woods had had a turn in the boat, and afterwards the official crew watched the boat from the bank while she was put through her paces by Miss Pamela Clabburn, crewed by another young lady. The trial was considered entirely satisfactory, and at a meeting of the Broads Motor Boat and Sailing Club, held in Norwich on Saturday, other members agreed to have dinghies built to the same plan and specification. The boats will all be of varnished mahogany clench built, copper fastened, with gunter rig, and

a sail area of 125 sq ft, no spinnaker being allowed. The aim is to eliminate complicated gear, and there is even no forestay. The mast and spars are of bamboo. The sail, which is of union silk, has no battens. Buoyancy tanks are fitted. It is expected that the new fleet will be racing at Easter."

The origins of the Norfolk dinghy parallels those of the famous 'X' OD in that both classes were sponsored by a Motor Yacht Club. It seems that Herbert Woods was quick off the mark, because at a meeting called by the Broads Motor Boat and Sailing Club to decide on a design for the new dinghy, it was suggested that Uffa Fox should be asked to submit plans, whereupon Woods produced a set of lines and specifications which he said he would be pleased to present to the Club.

Sailing open dinghies on the Norfolk Broads had been popular since before the turn of the century and in 1895 the Broads Dinghy Club was formed with a membership subscription of two shillings and sixpence. Their rules were simple:

"Boats to be open boats not exceeding fourteen feet overall, clench built, 140 feet of canvas to cover whole of sail area, no

The Norfolk Frostbite SC races on the river Bure in Norfolk 14ft ODs each winter between October and Easter. Here, *Joy* (B12) is almost planing under a reefed main.
Photo: Alan Mitchell

outside ballast, inside ballast not to exceed three hundredweight, centreplate (exposed) not to exceed four square feet and eighty pounds weight, and to be of a uniform thickness throughout. Rudder to be ordinary wood, rudder to unship. Outside fixed keel and deadwood together not to exceed three inches in depth, and the garboard strake to show inside the boat; draught exclusive of centre keels, not to exceed fifteen inches with crew and ballast on board. Crew not to exceed two persons."

Many lugsail boats of this kind were built during the first half of the century in yards around the Broads and judging by the recollection of one who took part in the Dinghy Club races of those days, they were robust events – *"There was no such thing as a protest in my young days. The crews landed on the bank and fought it out with their fists if there was any disagreement".*

It is clear from those boats that are still around, often known as 'Dumplings', that the simple rules of the Broads Dinghy Club were not sufficient to prevent enthusiastic owners from altering and improving their boats so that before long no two boats were alike. That is why the Norfolk OD dinghy

The Norfolk 14, *Chuph*, chasing *Bungle* (B75), *White Wings* (B32) and *Teal* (B2) round a bend in the Bure during the 1991 Class Jubilee Race. Photo: Paul Janes.

came into being. As forecast in the 'Eastern Daily Press', the first race for the Norfolk 14 footers was held on Easter Monday 1931 and was from Potter Heigham to Hickling Broad. There were six entries and the winner was *Swift* (No.3), one of the few boats that have been lost to the fleet, having migrated to Richmond on the Thames before the War and then becoming untraceable. A total of twelve boats were built in that first year. At the first A.G.M. of the Norfolk Dinghy Club, the secretary reported that the weights of some of the boats varied by as much as 29 lbs. When asked why this was, Herbert Woods replied – 'Because I don't grow the trees – that is the trouble. You can take the same plank and one end will weigh very much heavier than the other'.

Woods has always been the sole builder of Norfolk 14s, although some 'unauthorised' boats were built by Everson of Woodbridge on the Deben, where they came to be known as the Kingfishers. The lines were taken off *Whimbrel* (No. 33), while she was in store during the latter years of the War. *Whimbrel* is now back with the Norfolk fleet and the Kingfishers are no more.

As with every other one-design class, new rules for the Norfolk 14s were soon found

necessary. The first came after it had been noticed that some boats had their mainsails hoisted higher than normal and were picking up extra wind above the reeds and bushes bordering the Broads. A painted black band 3ft 6in above the mast-step soon put a stop to that.

Sails for the Class have always been made by Jeckells of Wroxham, who were allowed to switch from cotton to Terylene in the 1950s. The sliding gunter rig has been maintained throughout and the Norfolks have always spurned the spinnaker. They are not even allowed to use a poled-out jib. It was not until 1977 that jamming cleats and toe-straps were permitted. One unusual racing rule requires all boats to reef when reefing signals are hoisted. 'One cone beneath the Code flag 'U' for one reef and two cones beneath for two reefs in the mainsail. The reefing signal denotes the minimum number of reefs. Boats may reef if they wish when no signals are hoisted.'

Alan Mitchell, one-time Class captain has described a race on Oulton Broad with two reefs down :

"The wind was even stronger on Sunday and two reefs were ordered. I recall surfing down to the start line – the problem was

keeping the spray out of the boat – some boats had spray sheets but the others just baled and baled. The fleet kept well together for the first beat, but the long run to the next buoy produced a crop of problems. Tom Percival rolled over near the top of Breydon and finished up sitting on the wall with his crew, holding Windy *off with their feet.* Hanser *shipped so much water that Chris Wilson could not bring her round the leeward mark and hove-to, baling.* Joy *gybed on this mark and pulled out her port chain plate and capsized."*

In all, 86 Norfolk 14s were built, the last one in 1968, and all but five of them are still around. Some of the boats still racing regularly have been in the same hands or the same family for decades. Raymond

Jeckells has owned *Cockle* (No.11) since 1948, while Martin Broom has had *Tideway* (No. 59), since she was built in 1948. No new boats have been built in recent years because of the prohibitive cost, but several hulls have been partially or completely rebuilt – and that is how the fleet has been maintained. Unlike some other classes, the Committee of the Norfolk 14s has always voted against moulding in GRP.

The largest fleet is based on Wroxham Broad, where the Class held its Jubilee Regatta in 1981, but there are other fleets at Coldham Hall, Beccles, Hickling and Barton Broads. In the winter, the Norfolks race on the Yare under the flag of the Norwich Frostbite SC.

Winter sailing with two reefs.

Royal Burnham One-Design

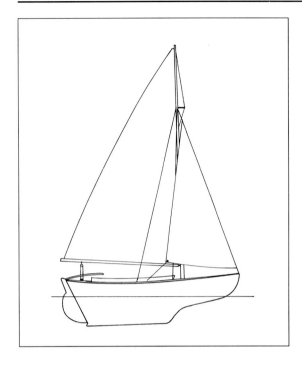

RB

Length Overall: 20ft (6.1m)
Length Waterline: 17ft 6in (5.3m)
Beams: 6ft 8in (2m)
Draught: 3ft 3in (1m)
Sail Area: 240 sq ft (22 sq m)
Designer: N. Dallimore
Builder: W. King & Sons.

Few people would know that the Royal Burnham Yacht Club held races on the river Crouch for the 12-metre Class until 1934, when three of the boats competed during Burnham Week. By that time the Club had already realised that the days of the 'big' Classes, including the West Solent Restricted Class they had sponsored since 1925, were ending and that they must look for a smaller one-design.

One proposal was the Star, and another favoured importing the well tried 'X' Class from the Solent. In the event it was decided to accept a 20ft keel boat designed by Norman Dallimore, a Burnham man. The Royal Burnham One-Design, as it was to be called, was a carvel-built Bermudan sloop with a transom stern and an iron keel weighing 1,000 lbs. At first it was hoped the boats could be built for no more than £100, but Dallimore warned that this would not be possible with a decent specification. So the limit was raised to £125 and by the end of 1932, the builders, William King of Burnham, had orders for nine boats.

The design of the boat was purchased by the Club and it was agreed that thereafter, a royalty of one guinea would be paid to the designer by members of the Club and three guineas for any non-members. It was also agreed that the Class could be adopted by the Colne Yacht Club at Brightlingsea, whose members ordered six boats to be built by Douglas ('Robbie') Stone.

In fact by the time the Brightlingsea boats were built, their owners had left the Colne Yacht Club because they didn't like the 18ft Brightlingsea One-Design the Club had introduced. The renegades formed the Pyefleet Yacht Club and the new 20-footers came to be known as the Pyefleet boats with the letters 'PF' on the peak of their mainsails. The Pyefleet Club didn't survive the War and the boats eventually found their way back to Burnham to join the Royal Burnham fleet.

Photo Opposite:
The normal crew of a Royal Burnham OD is three, but Belinda *had four on board on this fresh day in 1985. Photo: Coloryan*

The R.B.O.D., is not a particularly pretty boat when compared for example with the Dragon, which is almost 10 feet longer and yet has less beam. Nevertheless it is obvious that Dallimore's design served the Club's purpose very well, since even though only 23 boats were built, after sixty years an average of a dozen boats race each week-end during the season and some 18 R.B.O.Ds competed during Burnham Week in its centenary year.

The sail area of a R.B.O.D. totals 240 square feet, which originally included a roller jib that could be pulled around to serve as a kind of spinnaker as was done on the Essex ODs. The jib could also be reefed on its roller, but that was considered rather unsatisfactory and after the War the jib was hanked to a forestay and a normal spinnaker allowed.

Like the 'X' OD, the R.B.O.D. has maintained its local popularity while resisting rather than accepting change. There now seems to be enough traditionalists around to sustain interest in wooden boats with dated rigs and performance-limiting restrictions. This is probably because that way the cost of keeping a boat competitive remains reasonable, while the chances of it winning rest mostly with the skipper and crew – which is exactly why the one-design concept was introduced.

The Royal Burnham OD, *Vaurnine*, built by King & Sons at Burnham in 1933, bowling down the river Crouch in a fresh breeze. Photo: F.J. Armes.

Royal Corinthian One-Design

Length Overall: 22ft 8in (6.9m)
Length Waterline: 17ft (5.2m)
Beam: 6ft (1.8m)
Draught: 3ft 6in (1.1m)
Sail Area: 226 sq ft (21sq m)
Designer: H.C. Smith
Builder: Burnham Yacht Building Co

The Royal Corinthian Yacht Club, whose clubhouse at the seaward end of the waterfront at Burnham-on-Crouch is still as conspicuous as when it was built in 1931, had been in existence since 1872 and at one time or another has sponsored several different one-design classes. The first was established in 1895, when the Club was based at Erith, on the Thames. That one-design was by Linton Hope and the 20ft Dabchicks as they were called, must have been one of Hope's less successful boats, since they were found to capsize readily and were only raced as a class for a couple of years.

Next came a larger boat, designed by G.U. Laws of Burnham, where the Club had established a branch in 1911. In 1913, three of the new 30-footers were built by W. King and Son at Burnham, although their first race was held at Port Victoria on the Medway. By 1914, there were seven boats racing but when War broke out some of them were laid up at Port Victoria and the others at Burnham. After the War the boats raced at Burnham and in an attempt to widen interest, the Class was renamed the East Coast One-Design and was known as that for another sixty years, albeit with declining numbers.

Two East Coast One-Designs were still around in 1992, and occasionally raced against each other in Old Gaffers events. One of them, *Chittabob IV* remained gaff-rigged, while the other, *Joyce* has the Bermudan rig adopted in 1926.

By the mid 1930s, it had become clear that because of the Depression, it was very unlikely that many more 30-foot boats would be built simply for racing round the buoys. F.G. (Tiny) Mitchell was Commodore of the Royal Corinthian Yacht Club from 1932 until after the Second World War and one of the first things he did was to provide the impetus to introduce a new and smaller one-design class. No doubt the Royal Corinthian Yacht Club had watched the successful introduction of the Royal Burnham One-Design by the Club next door, and probably thought it time to follow suit.

Another reason for the new class was the need to provide employment for the shipwrights at local yards. With that aim in mind, the new boat was designed by Harry Smith who also owned the Burnham Yacht Building Company, where the first batch of boats was built. Smith's design was for a 22ft open cockpit boat with a beam of 6ft

Five Royal Corinthian ODs reaching down the Crouch. The three boats ahead are: *Coriander* (No.14), *Corsair* (No. 8) and *Cormorant* (No. 12). Photo: Trevor Davies

and a draught of only 3ft 6in. The carvel hull itself is shallow and flat bottomed, stability being provided by a fin keel carrying 8cwt. of lead. W. King and Son, another local yard, also built four boats while a further two were built by Stone at Brightlingsea. The boats built by the Burnham Yacht Building Company were planked 'upside down' on the first floor of the shed and then lowered to the ground and turned over before the wood and lead keels were added.

The first of the new R.C.O.D.s to get afloat was *Coral Nymph*, owned by Mrs V.M. Ogilvie, who lent her to members of the Club to try. By the next season, 1935, there was a fleet of fourteen boats, with names that all begin with the letters COR.

Like the Royal Burnham ODs next door, the Corinthian boats were originally Bermudan-rigged with a roller jib that could be poled out when sailing off the wind. They sailed like that until 1948, when Norman Dallimore redesigned the rig by replacing the roller sail with a hanked-on jib and adding a spinnaker. But it was not until 1957 that Terylene sails were allowed and 1970 before it was decided to accept metal masts.

Throughout its sixty years of existence the R.C.O.D. Class has keenly preserved its one-design characteristics. For example, so concerned has the Class Committee been to ensure uniformity in the fleet, that they not only require all boats to be launched on the same day and scrubbed only on certain prescribed dates, they also stipulate the type of anti-fouling paint that must be used. Even these precautions did not satisfy some owners, who believed that certain boats were becoming foul sooner than others. It happened that the International Paint Company had a research centre at Burnham, and their Chief Marine Chemist was able to arrange for the owners of R.C.O.D.s to receive paint from the same batch!

When it was introduced, the Class adopted a rather curious points system, whereby the winner of a race is awarded points equal to the number of starters plus one, while the second boat gets points equal to the number that started minus one, while everyone else gets one less right down the fleet. The Class is also unusual in that even now, in 1993, it holds no races on Sundays.

There was a time in the 1960s, when many people including yachting journalist Hugh Somerville, reckoned that GRP boats like the Ajax and the Scimitar would replace – 'some of the crumbling local keel-boat classes'. But before the end of that decade, Somerville had changed his mind, after sailing with Tony Cash in *Coryphee* and then writing another article in which he asked himself "Who said 'crumbling classes' anyway?"

Corindelle (No. 17), was the last of the Royal Corinthian One-Designs to be built, in 1936. Here she is racing on the Crouch in 1983. Photo: Coloryan

Victory Class

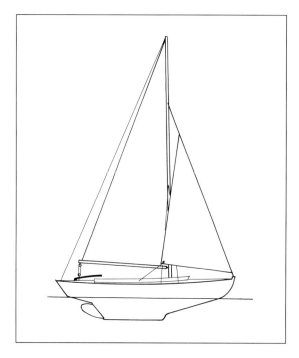

Z

Length Overall: 20ft 9in (6.3m)
Length Waterline: 16ft 9in (5.1m)
Beam: 5ft 10in (1.8m)
Draught: 2ft 6in (0.75m)
Sail Area: 145 sq ft (13 sq m)
Designer: C.E. Nicholson after S.N. Graham
Builders: Various

In 1934 a local newspaper reported that more than 200 small craft were kept in Portsmouth Harbour and that – 'where vigorous racing did exist, it came in the one-design classes, where a good number of competitors started and raced together on level terms. The Portchester Ducks Class is a fine example and some half-dozen former Bembridge one-design class boats race regularly in the harbour'.

It was in this climate that a group of local yachtsmen formed the Portsmouth Harbour Racing and Sailing Association and decided to establish a 'Harbour One-Design'. The first President of the new Association, Harry Brickwood, was a successful 'X' boat helmsman and it was not surprising that he recommended adoption of the Westmacott designed ex-Bembridge boat, particularly since there were several of them already in the harbour. The name chosen for the new class was Victory, no doubt because of the Navy's close involvement in those early days.

But there was an immediate problem because the drawings of the Bembridge OD had been lost in a fire at Woodnutt's yard on the Isle of Wight. So arrangements were made for a naval architect, Sidney Graham, to take the lines off one of the existing boats and to make a new set of drawings – for which he was paid ten guineas.

Then the Navy took a hand by allowing an ex-Chief Joiner to make a set of moulds while working in the Shipwrights shop of H.M.S. *Dolphin*. In fact the Navy played a prominent part in establishing the new Class and Commander H.M. Denham became the first Class Captain.

While the new drawings were being made, the opportunity was taken to make some modifications to Westmacott's original design. Firstly the centreplate was removed and replaced by 2cwt. of internal lead ballast while the overall length was increased slightly and the draught reduced to 2ft 6in. But perhaps more important, the rig was updated by Charles Nicholson who gave the Victory a Bermudan main with a small jib and a total sail area of 195 square feet.

All of the originally gaff-rigged boats were soon converted to the new rig, which then served the Class until 1969, by which time improved sail cloths had become available and were permitted. Then, the rig was again changed by abandoning running backstays and substituting a single standing backstay.

Two Victory Class ODs: *Zest* (Z30) and *Mistress* (Z16) on a fresh day in the Solent; circa 1946. Photo: Beken of Cowes

This meant shortening the boom and re-cutting the mainsail, the lost area of which was transferred to a larger foresail. Other 'modernisation' steps were the optional use of a centre-mainsheet and ratchet blocks, but not a metal mast.

In general Class rules for the Victory were, and are quite strict. Boats can only be built by approved builders, using the official templates. The first builder was Portsmouth based Harry Feltham who died suddenly, one evening in 1958 while at the helm of *Janet* (223). Later boats were built by Hamper of Fareham and more recently by John Perry of Southsea. Perry served his apprenticeship with Harry Feltham, so he is well used to building to the Victory class specification; although this has not prevented him (with the approval of the Class regulators) from introducing minor modifications in construction. The changes have all been aimed at producing a strong and more easily maintained boat. Nowadays the boats are normally planked in half-inch iroko, with laminated floors and knees and steamed American elm timbers. Transom and thwarts are of teak.

The Victory Class is distinctive in several ways. The sail insignia is a 'Z' and all the clench-built hulls are painted black with a distinctive boot-topping colour to indicate the club to which the owner belongs: green for the Royal Albert Yacht Club, scarlet for the Portsmouth Sailing Club, white for the Royal Naval Sailing Association and sky-blue for the Royal Air Force Yacht Club.

The Victory proved to be a seaworthy boat, although there have been some sinkings when boats have been caught in a squall with mainsheets made fast or when too much water had been allowed to swill about in the bottom of the boat.

Over nearly sixty years, more than 70 boats have been built, including Nick Chandler's 271 *Christina* and Andrew Storey's Z72 *Zingara*, both from John Perry's yard.

Since its inception nearly sixty years ago, the Victory Class has always raced at Cowes during the Week, and in 1991, as many as 35 boats competed there.

Photo Overleaf:
Zelia (Z54), *Simba* (Z29) and *Circa* (Z61) in a two reef breeze. Photo: Hamo Thornycroft

Hampton One-Design

Length Overall: 18ft (5.5m)
Length Waterline: 14ft (4.3m)
Beam: 5ft 9in (1.75m)
Draught: 8in (3ft 6in) – (0.2m & 1m)
Displacement: 500 lbs (min) (226kg)
Sail Area: 195 sq ft (18 sq m)
Designer: V.A. Serio
Builders: Various

The Hampton-One, as it is often called, can be seen as a smaller version of the Star, except that it is a centreboarder and not a keel boat.

In 1934, members of the Hampton Yacht Club near Norfolk, Virginia, on the lower Chesapeake Bay, decided that they needed a one-design boat that would be simple to build and therefore not too expensive. The Star, which had been around since 1911, was considered, but it's keel made it unsuitable for the shallow waters of the Bay. However, a local designer/builder, Vincent Serio, came up with an 18-foot hard-chine boat that could be built in solid timber, with cedar planking on oak frames and still sell at $325.

By the summer of 1935, the first seven boats were racing and by 1938, when 70 had been built, the Hampton-One Racing Association was formed. For many years the rules initially adopted for the Class were strictly enforced. Spars had to be solid pine or spruce and minimum weight was checked before every important event. After World War II, some wooden Hampton-Ones were built in Holland and imported into the US by Edward Wolcott, whose family have been keen supporters of the Class for several generations.

Like the Star, the Hampton-One has a large mainsail in relation to its hull size and until a trapeze was allowed in 1962, they must have been a handful in a blow. 1962 also saw the acceptance of GRP building and the use of bendy metal spars. The cost of building a Hampton One-Design in wood has become prohibitive and even a GRP version costs about $8000. But older wooden boats still change hands at around $2500.

It is clear that these old boats can still compete successfully, because first and second places from a fleet of twenty five in the 1992 National Championship were taken by wooden boats, one of them, *Calamity Jane*, having been built in 1948.

Like the Star, the 'Hampton One' as the Class is often called, has a very large mainsail so that in anything of a breeze, both helmsman and crew have to work hard to keep her upright. Photo: Scott Wolff

These Hampton ODs were competing in the fifty seventh National Championship of the Class in 1992. Photo: Ron Roblee

Royal Mersey 'Mylne' OD Class

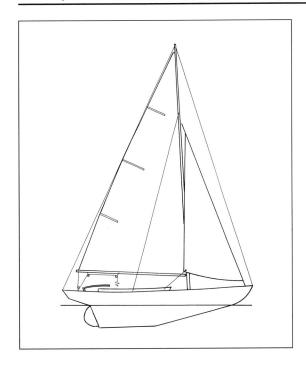

Length Overall: 24ft 10in (7.5m)
Length Waterline: 18ft (5.5m)
Beam: 7ft (2.1m)
Draught: 3ft 3in (1m)
Displacement: 4,600 lbs (2083kg)
Sail Area: 250 sq ft (23 sq m)
Designer: Alfred Mylne
Builders: Various

In 1935, prompted perhaps by the success of the Conway Yacht Club's 16ft Fife OD, the Royal Mersea Yacht Club and the Trearddur Bay Sailing Club jointly asked Alfred Mylne to design a somewhat similar boat for them. They wanted their boat to be 18ft on the waterline and therefore slightly longer than the Fife boat.

Ten years earlier, Mylne had designed a boat for a one-design class sponsored by the Royal Bombay Yacht Club and although slightly larger, that design was similar in many respects to the one he offered to the Royal Mersea YC

The Mylne 18-Footers, as the new class came to be called, drew only 3ft 3in; the same as the Fife-16s. The first five boats were built by Munro & Son at Blairmore in Scotland, but in 1936, permission was given for Dickie & Sons of Bangor to build five Mylnes for members of the Treaddur Bay Sailing Club. While all of the Royal Mersey Mylne boats have names beginning with MER-, the Treaddur boats had names that began with TR-.

The Mylne-18s were more heavily built than the Fifes, and they were also cheaper; costing only £180 in 1935. The rigs and sail plans of the two designs were very much the same and originally they carried almost the same area of sail.

By 1939, some 16 boats had been built to Mylne's design and seven of them belonged to members of the Royal Mersey YC

After the War there were more Mylne 18s sailing at Treaddur Bay than at the Royal Mersey, but in 1951, two of the Treaddur fleet were lost in a storm and others were damaged. After that the Mylnes never again sailed at Treaddur and the remainder of their fleet moved to Mersey, where most of them were renamed to comply with the MER- convention.

By the end of the 1960s, there were eleven Mylne-18s sailing as a Class, but no new boats were being built. So, just like the Fife Class Association before them, the Mylne Class Association eventually decided to allow GRP-built boats into the Class. In 1983, a mould was made taken from one of the original wooden hulls and the first GRP Mylne-18 was produced. Since then four others have followed and the future of the Class seems assured.

Although there is a difference of two feet between the waterline lengths of the two boats, the Fifes and the Mylnes regularly race against each other during the Menai Straits Regattas in August, when the Mylne boats can easily be distinguished by the Liverbird insignia on their sails. When he described the Mylne 18-Footers in his book 'Racing Cruising and Design', Uffa Fox forecast that – 'After studying these plans one is convinced that these little ships will be giving pleasure to their owners 40 years from now.' Uffa wrote that some 55 years ago.

These first five Mersey Mylne ODs were built in Scotland by Munro in 1935. No. 4 is hidden behind No. 1. Photo: Courtesy of Charles Kay

The Mersey Mylne OD, *Meridian*, beating towards the Menai Bridge. Photo: Ann Dowse.

Wivenhoe One-Design Class

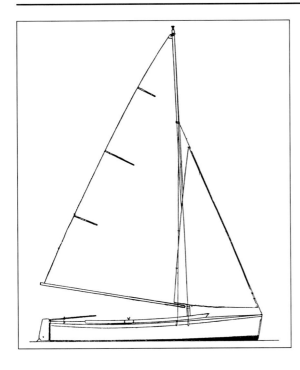

Length Overall: 15ft (4.6m)
Length Waterline: 15ft (4.6m)
Beam: 5ft 2in (1.6m)
Draught: 10in (3ft 6in)
- (0.2m & 1.1m)
Sail Area: 130 sq ft (12 sq m)
Designer: Dr. W. Radcliffe
Builders: Various

In the early 1930s, the Wivenhoe Sailing Club, based on the north bank of the river Colne, decided that they, like so many neighbouring clubs, should have a one-design boat to replace the miscellaneous craft that had been racing under handicap rules. There were several local classes that might have served them – the West Mersea Sprite or the Walton and Frinton Jewel – for examples; but the members of the Wivenhoe Club decided to use the talents of a local amateur designer.

With the help of members of the club, Dr. Water Radcliffe produced drawings and specifications for a 14ft, three-quarter-decked clench-built boat with a Bermudan rig and a sail area of 130 sq ft, plus a spinnaker.

Rather surprisingly, because Wivenhoe was a boat-building town, the first batch of six Wivenhoe OD hulls were built by Parsons at Leigh-on-Sea. They were strongly built with spruce planking on American elm frames and extra floors to allow them to take the ground safely twice a day. The boats were finished at Wivenhoe by a co-operative effort of their owners.

The first six boats soon attracted the favourable attention of members of the Stour Sailing Club at Manningtree and three of

their members ordered boats for sailing on the river Stour.

By the outbreak of World War II, the eighteen Wivenhoe ODs that had been built were distributed between Wivenhoe, Manningtree and Brightlingsea. After the War, a few boats began to race again at Wivenhoe, but the Class then went through a lean time throughout the 1960s and 70s. Then Malcolm Goodwin, a World Hornet Champion and owner of one of the original Wivenhoe ODs, suggested that a new Class Association should be formed. The purpose of the new Association, which was formed in 1980, was to recruit support for the Class from any previous owners or crews or anyone else who was interested in preserving the Class.

The idea worked and by 1985, the Jubilee year of the Class, all sixteen of the known existing boats were at Wivenhoe.

The story of the recovery of the Wivenhoe One-Design Class from its period of decline has been told by Walter Evans in a booklet published to celebrate the Jubilee year of the Class. Part of it is worth repeating here because it tells how enthusiasm and persistence can be combined to revitalize a class that might otherwise become defunct. The story began

Wivenhoe ODs racing on the river Colne during the Wivenhoe Regatta of 1935. The leading boat is *Ranger*. Photo: Courtesy of Malcolm Goodwin.

with the rebuilding of *Duet* (No.2):

"She had fallen 15 feet onto the concrete while being hoisted for winter storage onto the first floor of the Wilkins Jam Factory. Her bows were burst completely open, her fore-deck torn loose, the ends of her strakes shattered when they were ripped from the stem, and the stem itself smashed by the impact. Her loss was a serious blow to the fleet – only five boats at that time being left in commission at Wivenhoe, and of these only one or two turned out for club races.

During 1978, having failed to get any boatyard even to consider rebuilding her, her then owners, Cecily and Walter Evans, were introduced to Geoff Bailey, as being an amateur boat-builder and a professional expert in modern commercial glues. A quiet modest man, he made no promises or conditions – simply said he had looked at the remains of Duet *and said he felt he could make a boat out of them again. It took many hours of devoted work, but he succeeded brilliantly and she is now one of the soundest boats in the fleet and,*

remarkably for a clinker-built boat of her age, totally dry.

A newly formed W.O.D. Owners' Association decided that special efforts must be made to re-vitalise the Class. Members felt that the bringing back to life of Duet *supported their own conviction that the W.O.D. design was so basically good, and the contruction so thoroughly sound that if a boat so completely wrecked as* Duet *could be re-built, there was no reason why other boats which had left the district and were lying in a state of neglect could not be similarly restored. As a result of this upsurge of enthusiasm, several boats were found or enticed back to Wivenhoe. A great fillip to this process was given by* Elise *(No.17). She had been brought back from Brightlingsea to Wivenhoe by Pat Hatch and John Lay-Flurrie who raced her with great keenness, winning by a large margin the W.O.D. Cup, for points scored over the whole season. This had been presented by Cecily and Walter Evans to encourage W.O.D. racing, and was being competed for in that year for the first time.*

Fourteen Wivenhoe ODs reaching down the river Colne during a race in 1983.
Photo: Malcolm Goodwin

Chiquita *(No.15) had been found in a state of serious neglect at West Mersea, where she had been left upside down in the open without any cover, with her phosphor-bronze centreplate still in her, pulling her out of shape and bending her main thwart till it cracked. Through David Cannell's diplomacy we were able to buy her from the boat-yard concerned at scrap value, and Colin Butterfield undertook the mammoth task of restoring her shape and condition. Dorothy (No.9), which had been away for some years was brought back from Manningtree under an agreement with her owner, Dr Erskine.* Osprey *(No.19) was brought back to the Colne. Then* Capriol *(No.11), which had originally been owned by Dr. Water Radcliffe, the designer of the W.O.D. Class, and thus of particular significance, had been located lying on the mud at Tollesbury. Her mast had been left lying on the ground, had rotted and was in two halves: she had no boom or*

rudder but her deck and planks appeared sound, and she still had her original phosphor-bronze centreplate. So we added her to the fleet, which now numbered 10 boats.

In the spring of 1979, Nick Baker found a note attached to his W.O.D., Vivian *(No 4) at Rowhedge. The writer of the note said he thought he had the hull of a sister-yacht, lying at Gosport on the South Coast. She had lost mast, boom and rudder when a gale blew her under a pier some time back, but she was now floating at a mooring. Pat Hatch, who had to visit the south coast on business had a look at her, confirmed that she was in fact a W.O.D. and brought her back with him. She was stripped of a very heavy crop of barnacles and weed and a cargo of mud, crabs and a six-inch starfish, and there was a prolonged debate as to her identity. This was eventually confirmed by Ernie Vince, who had sailed extensively in her, as* Corretta *(No. 16)."*

113

Menai Straits One-Design

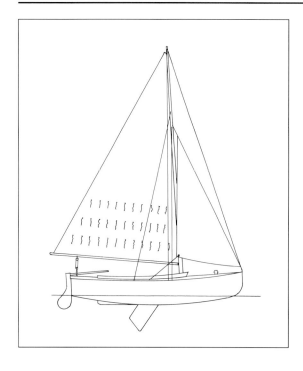

MS

Length Overall: 20ft (6.1m)
Length Waterline: 20ft (6.1m)
Beam: 6ft 9in (2m)
Draught: 9in (3ft 6in) – (0.2m & 1.1m)
Sail Area: 212 sq ft (20 sq m)
Designer: W.H. Rowland
Builder: Morris and Leavett

In 1936 W.H. Rowland who had been responsible for the Conway OD in 1928, designed a square stem and stern 20 foot three-quarter-decked, carvel-planked, centreboarder to carry 212 square feet of sail with a crew of three. Seventeen of these boats were built between 1937 and 1951 by Morris & Leavett of Beaumaris and some were sailed before World War II by cadets from the training ship H.M.S. *Conway*. After the War, during the 1960s and 70s, the Class almost expired, but then Raymond Beer set about recovering and arranging the restoration of several of the boats that had been sold away from North Wales. The result of his and other enthusiasts' efforts is that there are now enough Menai Straits ODs to race together as a class during the annual Straits Regattas.

The way in which one of the boats – *Sudy* (No. 14) was recovered from dead, has been described by Steward Warburton, who found her after she had been converted to a cruiser:- ". . . complete with cabin, alloy spars, inboard engine, triple keels and worse still, fibreglass sheathing". He recalls that – "When I first saw her with her peeling paint, dangling strands of sheathing and caulking, twisted stem and wet rot, I wrote her off as an impossible restoration proposition". But then

he adds – "Something, however kept drawing me back to Gallows Point where she rested on the club cradle. Despite her years of neglect, she had not lost her lines and her planks seemed in reasonable condition, so one fine morning I arrived with notepad, tape measure and spike".

Warburton bought *Sudy* for £150 in 1985 and on June 24th 1989 she raced again in her class.

This shot of *Suzanne,* Menai Straits OD No. 3, was taken off Beaumaris in 1987.
Photo: William Rowntree

Photo on left page:
The Menai Straits OD Class boats *Gwylan* (No. 4) and *Jetemaan* (No.7) race neck and neck during the Conway YC Regatta in 1980. The Mersey Mylne OD in the background is *Mersey,* one of the first boats to be built in that Class.
Photo: William Rowntree.

Loch Long One-Design

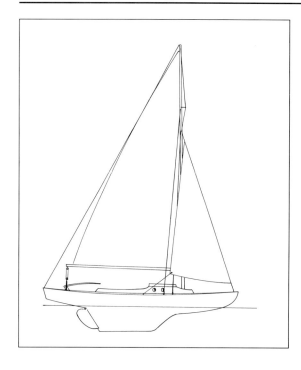

LL

Length Overall: 21ft (6.4m)
Length Waterline: 15ft 3in (4.6m)
Beam: 5ft 10in 1.8m)
Draught: 2ft 8in (0.8m)
Displacement: 1200 lbs (544kg)
Sail Area: 160 sq ft (15 sq m)
Designer: J Croll after J.Jacobsson
Builders: Various
Portsmouth Yardstick: 123

The design of the Loch Long has been attributed to different people, 'Lloyds Register' simply saying – 'Norwegian Design – Modified'. In 'Yachting Monthly' for November 1949 a photograph of a boat is accompanied by the caption : 'Among the many one-design classes that race regularly North of the Border one of the most successful is the Loch Long Class, known in their local Clyde waters as the "Wee Dragons" since the design shows several of the characteristics of the Dragons.' Yet in Sir Peter Johnson's 'Encyclopedia of Yachting', it is recorded that Charles Nicholson was the designer.

As is so often the case, the true story is complex. It seems that in 1936 the members of the Loch Long Sailing club had become dissatisfied with the sport they were getting with their fleet of handicap dinghies. Following a visit to Scandinavia, one of the club members, Ian Campbell, returned with the plans of a boat that had been designed by Janne Jacobsson of Gothenburg just before the First World War. The Stjärnbät (Starboat) was originally a half-decked, clench-built 18-footer with a transom stern and a fin keel. The pre-War boat was gaff-rigged but by updating the class to Bermudan rig in 1928, its

popularity was maintained and more than a thousand boats were built, with some four hundred still sailing in Scandinavia.

But most of the members of the Loch Long Club didn't much like the Stjärnbät – mainly because of its transom stern. So one of them, James Croll, introduced some modifications; adding a counter and a small cuddy as well as calling for carvel rather than clench fastened planking. The greater length also allowed the use of a standing backstay for the Bermudan rig. There is no record that the original designer ever objected to the modification of his boat, but on the other hand it may have been some time before anyone in Sweden knew what had happened.

Croll must have been very keen on the boat he had partly created, because he offered to put up the money required to build the first five boats. An initial batch of five were built because Robert Colquhoun of Dunoon reckoned that he could not keep the price down to £66 per boat for any smaller order. Apart from No. 2 *Rumajo*, which was retained by Croll for his three daughters to sail, the other four boats were jointly owned by two or more local yachtsmen and the first race was held on the day the boats were launched

The Loch Long OD, *Finola*, in a jump of a sea. The helmswoman is Isobel Napier and the shot was taken in the 1950s. Photo: Ian Gilchrist.

In 1992 there were twenty Loch Long ODs at Aldeburgh in Suffolk. Here, one of them reaches a mark just ahead of a Squib. Photo: Coloryan

– Coronation Day, Wednesday May 12th 1937.

In the following year, Croll caused a stir by having Colquhoun build him a second Loch Long with lighter planking and a heavier keel. *Minx* as she was called, cost £130, which was almost twice as much as had been paid for the other boats. Not unreasonably, *Minx* was not allowed to race in the class and in fact she was never registered until 1946.

Colquhoun was the only builder of Loch Longs before the War and he died in 1940. Also in that year the original plans for the boat were lost in a fire, so that after the War, a new set of lines had to be lifted from an existing boat – *Roma*. This was done firstly by Robert Shaw of Cove, who subsequently built eight boats in all.

Another set of 'official' lines were taken off *Roma* by James Rodgers of Glasgow on behalf of the newly formed Loch Long Owners Association. William Boag of Largs, with a total of 65 boats, built most Loch Longs, while Robertsons of Sandbank built 27. In 1963, Boag was charging £496 for a basic, mahogany-planked boat complete with a suit of cotton sails. Terylene sails from Ratsey cost an extra £32-14s.

Altogether, eleven different yards have built Loch Longs, so it is rather unlikely that all the existing boats would pass strict measurement tests. Major differences seem to have been in the weight of keels. In 1950, a debate started that threatened the future of the Class. The dispute centred around a claim that eight boats built by Robertsons during 1949/50 had keels weighing 700 lbs. as against the 640 lbs of more recent boats. The principal complainant was James Rodgers, who had lifted the lines off *Roma*, and had built three boats with the lighter keels. Among the objections Rodgers raised, were that: 'We have now turned out to have three distinct classes instead of one-design. We have the original Loch Long boat, which due to its shape and construction materials could not advantageously carry the weight as now proposed. We have the spruce boats (Robertsons) which violated the specification in every conceivable form and which, to my mind, cannot have a valid certificate, especially so since the weight is now divulged at 732 lbs, and thirdly we have the boat which was built of mahogany, or similar timbers of a heavier weight ratio, and carrying the 640 lbs keel.'

Rodgers proposed that the Class should be divided and that the spruce planked boats should forfeit the Loch Long name; but his suggestion was rejected and the argument continued. Eventually, at a meeting of owners in 1952, it was concluded that the extra weight did not give any clear advantage and the eight suspect boats should remain in the Class. It would seem that in some of the fleets, all three types of boat are still sailing together. Certainly that is the view of John Haig, owner of a Loch Long at Aldeburgh, who said in 1992 'We have a class of Loch Longs at Aldeburgh which are not exactly one-design – there seem to be several designs in fact'.

The Loch Longs at Aldeburgh increased from six to twenty boats towards the end of the 1980s, some of them owned by erstwhile owners of Dragons, of which there is a strong local fleet. This tendency by those who are no longer as nimble as they once were, to switch to a smaller less demanding boat

have led to the Loch Longs being nicknamed 'Geriatric Dragons.'

The first official proposal to allow spinnakers to be used in the Class was made in 1949 and it was still being debated in 1956, when a Col. Hunt from the Aldeburgh fleet argued that spinnakers are a bad thing for two reasons:

"One is that the Loch Longs are a very active class here, racing on Tuesday nights, Thursday nights and Saturday afternoons plus any odd races they can squeeze in. . . . It was felt that spinnakers would possibly debar quite a number of boats racing in the evenings as a more experienced type of crew would be required.

The second reason is that of expense. The original idea of the class was to provide a cheap racing boat for working-class people at Cove."

A third reason for Hunt's objection may have been the apprehension felt by the older members of the Aldeburgh Yacht Club who did not fancy having to deal with a recalcitrant spinnaker on the tiny foredeck of a Loch Long. Anyway, spinnakers are still not allowed in the Class on the Alde, even though they were adopted by all the other fleets.

As for glassfibre construction, the Loch Long Owners Association may well have been first to state the oft repeated proverb that – 'if God had intended us to sail in fibreglass boats he would have grown fibreglass trees'.

The 1960s were the most productive years for the Class, with some eighty-five boats being built during that decade. Since then the number of new boats each year has declined, no doubt because of the increased cost of building them. However, by 1990, despite the migration of boats to Aldeburgh, three fleets, numbering some 50 boats were sailing at the Royal Gourock YC, the Cove SC, and the Largs SC, where the Class began.

A new Loch Long (No. 153) was built for John Bartholomew by the Boatbuilding Training College at Lowestoft in 1991/2; albeit by using the keel taken from *Gazelle* who was too far gone to re-build. The new boat is called *Mosquito* and after being launched at Aldeburgh, she has returned to Scotland.

Royal Harwich One-Design

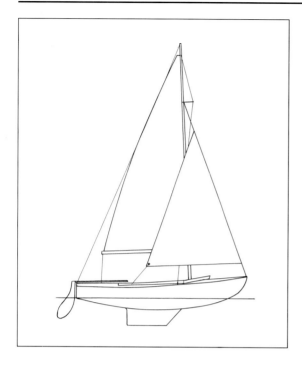

Length overall: 20ft (6.1m)
Length Waterline: 17ft 6in (5.3m)
Beam: 6ft 10in (2.1m)
Draught: 3ft (0.9m)
Sail Area: 217 sq ft (20 sq m)
Designer: Robert Clark
Builder: Sittingbourne
Shipbuilding Co.

In 1936, Sir William Burton, helmsman of Sir Thomas Lipton's *Shamrock IV* in the *America's* Cup races of 1920 and past President of the Royal Harwich Yacht Club, offered financial help in establishing a one-design class which he hoped would be adopted by the various clubs on the rivers Orwell and Stour.

There had been an earlier class of one-designs – the Orwell Corinthians – since 1899. They had been designed by H.C. Smith of Burnham-on-Crouch, but their popularity had declined and they were in poor shape; although one of them, *Raffles*, has been beautifully restored by Bruce Moss and now races with the Royal Harwich ODs.

The Royal Harwich OD, *Sandpiper* sailing off Pin Mill on the river Orwell.
Note the sounding pole. Photo: Coloryan

Led by Frank Tempest, a group of members of the R.H.Y.C. decided that what they needed was a – 'sea-going boat of modest size and price' and that they would commission the design of a boat of about 20ft.

Robert Clark was working in London with the firm of Clark and Synott and was yet to become famous for offshore yachts like the metacentric Mystery class. Clark delivered a set of lines for a 20ft carvel planked, three-quarter-decked boat with a ballasted fin-keel.

Several possible builders were approached, and the lowest quotation – £113 plus 6 Guineas designer royalty – from the Sittingbourne Shipbuilding Company, was accepted.

This choice of a barge-building yard to produce small yachts was surprising and gave rise to some subsequent criticism. Anyway, a batch of seven boats was ordered and an eighth was built 'on spec'. They were planked in Philippine mahogany, apparently because that timber was cheaper than the Honduras variety. By all accounts they were poorly finished, so that a great deal of further work was considered necessary and was carried out by Harry King after the boats reached Pin Mill. The slightly curved sheer line intended by the designer was also lost by the builder. Six of the seven boats were towed to the Orwell behind a motor boat, but *Miranda* (No.4), was sailed there in stages. The first leg was from Kings Ferry in the Swale to Burnham-on-Crouch and as his crew, Robert Clark had Austin, 'Clarence' Farrar, who was also working for Clark and Synott at the time. Austin Farrar has told of the voyage across the Estuary:

"We left King's Ferry early to catch the tide, Miranda *had been brought down the creek from Sittingbourne the previous day, and Robert Clark and I spent the night at the ferryman's house. Dawn saw very little wind but the first of the ebb took us down the Swale and out into Whitstable Bay clear of the Isle of Sheppey, where we picked up a pleasant sailing breeze to take us across the Thames estuary to skirt the Maplin sands on the north side of the Whitaker beacon, with the last of the ebb.*

The tide turned to help us up the Crouch, which was just as well as the wind was against us, and we got in some practise of short tacking. We found we were overtaking the local Burnham and Corinthian One-Designs which were having their Saturday afternoon races, and realised we had got quite a fast boat. We left Miranda *on one of Pettigrew's moorings and the following weekend another crew sailed her round to the Orwell."*

The new boats had a tall Bermudan rig that was quite modern for the time, with a forestay going to three-quarters of mast height and a standing topmast backstay with no runners. Booms were set high so that 'they didn't knock your hat off'. The upper mast was kept straight by 45 degree jumper struts and stays made from non-stretch 'piano' wire, an idea borrowed from dinghies like the International 14s. A spinnaker was allowed from the outset, but it was 1948 before sheet winches were permitted, and echo sounders are still excluded.

The first official sailmaker was Cranfield and Carter of Burnham, but when it was decided to consider switching from cotton to Terylene in the early 1970s, a single suit of new sails was ordered from Seahorse Sails, Austin Farrar's company in Ipswich. Those new sails were used throughout one season by each boat in turn, before the new material was accepted.

That all of the original boats are still sailing as a Class is a tribute to their designer and to those members of the Royal Harwich who saw the value of a small boat that would allow them – 'To race around the Cork Lightship and be home for afternoon tea.'

The well known designer and sailmaker, Austin Farrar, at the helm of *Jane*,
his Royal Harwich OD, built in 1937.
Photo: Coloryan

International One-Design

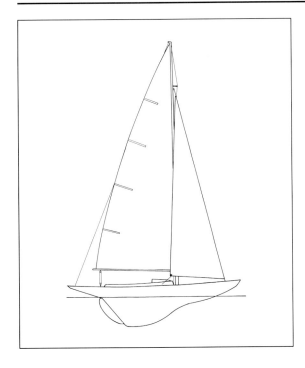

Length Overall: 33ft 4in (10.1m)
Length Waterline: 21ft 6in (6.5m)
Beam: 6ft 9in (2m)
Draught: 5ft 4in (1.6m)
Displacement: 6,950 lbs (3148kg)
Sail Area: 418 sq ft (38 sq m)
Designer: Bjarne Aas
Builder: Bjarne Aas until 1973

In the US, classes of large one-design yachts have flourished since the early years of this century. One of the most famous was the New York Yacht Club's Thirty-Foot Class – the thirty referring to waterline length. Eight of these Herreshoff-designed boats were built in 1905 and although they were exactly alike in every particular, the owners still drew lots for them. The New York Thirties raced very successfully for three decades, but in 1935 the members of the Club switched their allegiance to the Stevens-designed and Nevins-built New York 32s.

At about that time, Cornelius Shields, who had sailed in all kinds of craft from the 'J' Class yachts *Columbia* and *Yankee* down to Frostbite dinghies, happened to see a new 6-metre class yacht called *Saga*, that had been designed and built in Norway by Bjarne Aas.

In his book 'Racing, Cruising and Design', Uffa Fox described *Saga* as 'one of the best hard-weather sixes yet built' and 'Corny' Shields fell in love with her. But Shields realised that to own and race a boat in the International Six-Metre Class was a very expensive business, and he felt that something should be done to make it possible to race in similar boats without it costing as much.

His idea was to establish a truly one-design class designed by Bjarne Aas along the lines of *Saga*, but built in quantity in order to reduce costs. A request was sent to Aas to prepare a design for a semi-displacement boat about 33ft overall, with a beam of 6ft 9in, a draught of just over 5 ft and a small cabin – not unlike a large Dragon.

After minor modifications the design was approved and Shields, together with a group of like-minded friends, formed a syndicate to underwrite construction of 25 boats – an unusual undertaking. It was Shields' brother Paul who suggested calling the Class the International One-Design.

In so far as the Class has never been recognised by the IYRU, the name International One-Design is really a misnomer and recognising this, Uffa Fox more correctly sometimes referred to the boats as the Bjarne Aas One-Design.

In order to ensure that all the boats were the same, the syndicate employed a firm of Norwegian marine surveyors – the equivalent of Lloyds – to supervise building throughout. The cost of the first twenty five boats worked out at only $2,670 each, including sails, a cradle and shipping charges.

Some of the early I.O.D.s sailing off Bermuda. Circa 1938. Photo: Bermuda News Bureau

The sail plan of the I.O.D. calls for what today would be called a fractional rig, with the mast stayed with the aid of two sets of cross-trees and a pair of jumper struts – like a Dragon, but without running backstays.

From the outset, the rules were drawn up with the intention of keeping it a strictly controlled Class and some of the restrictions are interesting, for instance:

"Masts shall not be altered in their rake or position beyond limitations allowed by the opening in the mast partner" and *"Only one suit of sails (whether new or old) may be added to a boat's racing equipment in any one season"*. Again: *"During the life of any season's official racing schedule yachts*

shall not be hauled out or put on the beach more than once in three weeks and then for not more than ninety-six hours, subject to tides" and *"As a means of regulating the hoist of the mainsail, all boats must be equipped with a special shackle substantially 3in long."*

Uffa Fox, after an exciting race on the Solent in the I.O.D. *Windflower*, levelled a slight criticism, saying : 'Had I one of these lovely little vessels, I would ask permission to extend the rudder post above deck, as this would increase the length of the tiller, give you more leverage, and at the same time put the tiller up on deck where a man could exert his full strength on it comfortably'.

The current fleet of I.O.D.s at Bermuda are mainly GRP boats. Here, two of them are seen competing for the Omega Gold Cup in 1991. Photo: Bob Fisher

The new Class was a success in the US., with fleets being quickly established at Marblehead, on Long Island Sound and at San Francisco. Other fleets were started in Bermuda and in Sweden and Norway, where by 1939, Bjarne Aas had built 130 of the boats. In the UK, 'Tiny' Mitchell, Commodore of the Royal Corinthian Yacht Club had an I.O.D. named *Windflower* shipped to Burnham on Crouch in 1937, where she and three others, costing £445 each, raced until the outbreak of war in 1939 and again from 1946 until 1949. After that the Burnham boats, which had taken on the title of Royal Corinthian One-Designs, migrated to the newly formed branch of the Royal Corinthian Yacht Club at Cowes where a strong fleet of them formed the backbone of Club racing for several more years. At that time members of the Royal Corinthian were so keen on the

Class that they even persuaded Bjarne Aas to allow boats to be built in the UK, but in the event the concession was never exercised. Some of Frank Beken's very best photographs were of International One-Designs racing in the Solent during the 1950s.

Thereafter interest in the Class on the Solent began to decline and, as so often happens with one-design classes, other Clubs in different parts of the country took a fancy to the design and in 1972 the I.O.D.s migrated first to the Royal Forth YC at Granton and then across to the Royal Northern and Clyde YC at Rhu.

In the late 1960s, when GRP construction was growing, Bjarne Aas made a couple of plugs for I.O.D.s to be moulded in glass reinforced plastic, but only a few were built in this way. Then, in 1973 the Norwegian yard decided to cease building I.O.D.s. The ones he had built must have been well constructed because 21 of them were still sailing in Norway in 1992.

After that the GRP plugs were shipped to the USA and the rights to the design were purchased by the Class Association. But then, in 1979 after half a dozen hulls had been produced, they and the plugs were lost or damaged in a fire.

Fortunately one of the hulls could be repaired and used to make two new plugs – one of which was sent to Bermuda.

Since then all new I.O.D.s have been made from GRP and they are sailing alongside some of the restored wooden boats that were built before World War II.

It was always the intention of Cornelius Shields that contests sailed in I.O.Ds would be held in any of the centres having a fleet of the boats, without the visitors needing to take anything more than their personal belongings. On arrival in Norway, Bermuda or the US, they would simply draw lots for a boat, which in any case they would exchange for others during the series of races.

This rather ambitious scheme worked in 1990, when the Royal Northern and Clyde Yacht Club were hosts for the Class World Championship and again in 1992, when the Omega Gold Cup series of match races were sailed in I.O.D.s at Hamilton, Bermuda.

There is a fleet of a dozen I.O.D.s, several of them wooden, based at the Royal Northern and Clyde YC at Rhu in Scotland. In 1990, the Club organised the Class World Championship, visiting helmsmen sailing in the local boats, as Cornelius Shields, founder of the Class, had envisaged. Photo: Lean-Vercoe

Bembridge Redwing

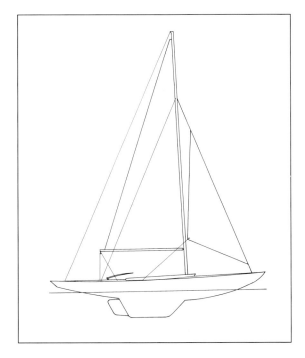

Length Overall: 27ft 11 in (8.5m)
Length Waterline: 20ft (6.1m)
Beam: 5ft 6in (1.7m)
Draught: 3ft 4in (1m)
Sail Area: 200 sq ft (18 sq m)
Designer: C.E. Nicholson
Builder: Camper & Nicholson

There are none of the original Redwings still racing as a Class and indeed it could be argued that neither those 1896 boats nor the 'new' Redwing introduced in 1938, should be considered proper one-designs, since from the outset their class rules have allowed an optional sail plan. Nevertheless, both the old and the new hull designs by Charles Nicholson, the famous designer of 'J' Class yachts, were so strictly controlled, that it is perhaps excusable to include them. For the first few years even the finish of the hull was specified, with black varnish being stipulated for use on the bottom.

The Redwing Club was established on the Solent in 1896 by members of the Royal Victoria Yacht Club and the Bembridge Sailing Club, and like the slightly earlier Water Wag Association, it was formed with the express purpose of sponsoring a particular class of boat. Some members of the Royal Victoria Yacht Club of Ryde and the Bembridge Sailing Club met with the object of 'starting a class of small boats for amateur racing, the half-raters having become too expensive and too soon outclassed for many to care to build'.

The first Redwing had an overall length of 22ft 1in and a waterline length of 16ft. A maximum beam of 5ft 5in and a waterline beam of only 4ft 7in indicates the 'peg-top' section of the carvel-planked hull,which drew 3ft. Stability was provided by a half-ton cast-iron keel, which also took the strains of the bumping and grounding the boats inevitably suffered in the shoal waters of Bembridge Harbour.

From the outset, the rig of a Redwing has been optional and during the early years of the Class many different shapes and arrangements of sails were tried – the only restriction being a maximum total area of 200 square feet.

Most of the experimental rigs were recorded by Frank Beken and many of his photographs are displayed on the walls of the Redwing Club at Bembridge. Among the rigs tried in the early years were the balanced lug sloop, gunter lug sloop, gaff mainsail sloop and square headed gaff sloop. For a while the favoured arrangement, was the Bembridge rig, which used a combined gaff and topsail together with a small headsail. Then came a period when the gaff rig was preferred, although balanced lugsails sometimes came out top at the end of the season. The first

Almost all of the Bembridge fleet of Redwings are GRP boats and there is no longer very much experimentation with different rigs – as the rules allow.
Photo: Hamo Thornycroft

Bermudan or Marconi rig was tried just before the 1914 War, but did not begin to take over until the 1920s. By 1934, *Fortuna*, one of the original fourteen boats, was the only one still using the gaff rig.

In 1937, by which time many of the Redwings were more than forty years old, the Club decided to replace their boats with a new design, again by Charles Nicholson and still to use sails with a maximum area of 200 square feet. The new boats were longer overall and on the waterline, but were more easily driven so retention of the old limit to sail area was possible.

The differences in construction between the old and new Redwings were noted by Uffa Fox in his 'Thoughts on Yachts and Yachting'. In particular he drew attention to the bent timbers of the old boats running down to the keel and being joined by galvanised iron floors and compared them with the canoe-like body of the new boats with its wood and lead keels bolted to it, the timbers being joined by wooden floors.

Uffa, who enthusiastically supported the concept of an optional rig on a strictly controlled one-design hull, experimented with the rig in *Ibis*, giving her as he said – 'the tallest and narrowest rig I imagined these Redwings could stand'. A similar, more successful and not quite so tall Bermudan rig was used in *Redstart*, who topped the Class in the first season's racing. Since then,

apart from a few excursions into the Lungstrom rig and rotating masts, most of the Redwing fleet have been using tall, narrow Bermudan mainsails with headsails that overlap but slightly, because they represent only about one third of the total sail area.

Uffa Fox summed up the spirit of sailing a Redwing when he wrote: *"Whenever we watch the bright sails of this class dancing over the Solent seas in a race, we not only witness a lovely spectacle of people enjoying the sunshine and fresh air in well designed and built little craft, but also having demonstrated before our eyes valuable lessons in the art of designing efficient rigs."*

At one time the Redwing fleet was limited to twenty boats, but that rule was relaxed and by 1990 there were some twenty-eight boats at Bembridge. Most likely the increased numbers were due to the decisions, made in 1988, to dispose of a number of the 1938 wooden boats and to build fifteen new boats of glass reinforced plastic. These decisions were not unanimously approved and at least one member, Vernon Stratton, proceeded to restore *Red Gauntlet*, using the West Epoxy System, and then went on to win six of the races during Cowes Week 1990.

Ten of the boats sold away from Bembridge went to Poole Harbour, where they continued their racing careers by being chartered to clubs, associations or individual groups.

National Redwing

R

Length Overall: 14ft (4.3m)
Length Waterline: 14ft (4.2m)
Beam: 5ft (1.5m)
Draught: 9in (5ft) – (0.2m & 1.5m)
Displacement: 275 lbs (Hull min)
(124kg)
Sail Area: 145 sq ft (No spinnaker)
(13 sq m)
Designer: Uffa Fox
Builders: Various
Portsmouth Yardstick: 116

In 1938, after having had four local boat-builders produce a centreboard dinghy that they considered suitable for sailing off the coast of Looe in Cornwall, the Commodore of the Looe Sailing Club, Wilfred Neale, decided to reject them all and go to Uffa Fox instead. The brief was for a one-design dinghy that would do well in the choppy waters of Looe Bay.

Uffa came up with a fourteen-foot part-decked clinker-built boat, the lines of which owed something to the International Fourteen footers. But unlike that International Class, the new boat was to be strictly one-design.

Neale liked what Uffa offered, and being a wealthy and generous man, he ordered eight boats from the Looe builders whose designs he had rejected earlier, keeping R1, *Jackdaw* for himself and presenting the other seven to people living in Looe. At that time each boat cost £47-10s, including sails. The Looe Redwing, as it was originally called, is 14ft overall with a beam of 5ft – slightly more than most International Fourteens – and at first the rules called for a metal drop-keel weighing 132 lb. Although it has 20 square feet more sail area than the International Fourteen, the Redwing is sturdily built,

weighs 150 lbs more than the Fourteen and is not allowed a spinnaker.

World War II prevented further building but the Redwing's popularity had been well established in the two years before the War, so that in 1946 the Class was adopted by the West of England Conference and then became known as the West of England Redwing. At this point yards outside Looe were allowed to build to the design, although Uffa Fox retained the copyright. After that it was not long before fleets of Redwings were established at Plymouth, Falmouth, Torbay and Penzance, with more than twenty boats at each centre. During the 1950s the Class continued to spread, with one fleet being established as far away as Hong Kong and others at Fishguard where the national Championship was held in 1991, and Tenby.

In the 1960s some changes were made to the Class rules, allowing the use of Terylene sails and a wooden centreboard in place of a metal centreplate or drop-keel. Uffa had given the Redwing a heavy cast-iron or mild steel centreplate and had always made it clear that this drop-keel made it possible for the Redwing to sail safely under conditions at sea that would capsize an

International Fourteen with a wooden centreboard. Uffa was therefore quite upset when he learned that the Class rules had been changed to allow the use of a buoyant wooden board in place of the 132 lb plate he had stipulated. Since he retained the copyright, Uffa threatened legal action, claiming damages of £10,000 because his design had been 'prostituted'. The argument continued until Uffa died and the rights to the design passed to the RYA.

Uffa's displeasure probably reflected just how pleased he was that in 1958, while metal drop-keels were still being used, Redwing R179 *Nimbus*, sailed by Neville Noye and Richard Parrott had won the Cross Channel dinghy race from Folkestone to Boulogne.

The RYA took over when the West of England Conference was disbanded in 1954, after which the Class became the RYA National Redwing.

It did not take long for those who had made the change to a wooden centreboard to discover that in a fresh wind without an iron plate the Redwing is soon overpowered unless the crew can get the whole of his body outboard. So, in 1976, taking a leaf out of the International Fourteen's book, the Class rules were changed to permit the use of a trapeze.

In 1979 trials were made with a spinnaker, but the experiment was considered a failure so the Redwing is now the only two-man dinghy that can use a trapeze but not a spinnaker. In 1984, metal masts were permitted but a resolution to allow GRP construction was never pursued. Whether this was a good thing depends upon one's point of view, but very few new boats have been built in recent years, although the number still on the register was well over 200 in 1991.

A group of National Redwing ODs racing at Looe in the early 1960s. Photo: Jonah Jones

Twenty-Three Lightnings at the start of a race on Lake Jacomo. This was taken before the Class numbered 10,000 boats. By 1993, the total had reached almost 15,000.
Photo: Courtesy of the Lightning Class Association

and 4ft 11in with it down. The combined sail area of the main and jib, is a modest 177 square feet, but a 300 square foot spinnaker provides plenty of excitement down wind. Although the Lightning could hardly be described as a high performance boat, a lot of first class helmsmen, including Dennis Conner have gained experience in them.

The Lightning has even been somewhat unkindly described as 'a flower box with a pointed end', but there must be more to it than that to explain the 15,000 'flower boxes' that have been registered during the fifty odd years since the first one was built. Of course today's boats, most of which are made from glass reinforced plastic materials, have far more rig and sail adjustments than the early boats.

Nevertheless, the one-design rules for the hull have been strictly enforced throughout the years so that older boats are still capable of winning top-class events.

It is generally acknowledged that the outstanding success of the Lightning Class is due to its excellent organisation. A single paid secretary, operating out of Worthington, Ohio, is supported by a team of voluntary officers located in many countries, so that World championships have been held in such widespread venues as Argentina, Finland, Switzerland, Ecuador, Canada and of course the US.

The Class has never been adopted in the UK, perhaps because a similar, although somewhat smaller boat – the Wayfarer – was introduced in 1958 to serve much the same purpose as the Lightning.

A 300-square-foot spinnaker makes the Lightning an exciting boat to sail in a breeze.
Photo: Courtesy of the Lightning Class Association

International 110 Class

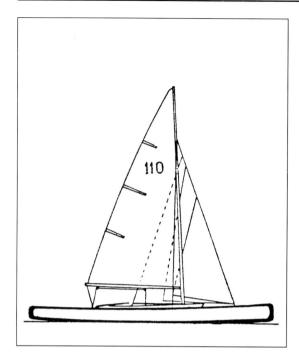

110

Length Overall: 24ft (7.3m)
Length Waterline: 17ft 6in (5.3m)
Beam: 4ft 2in (1.3m)
Draught: 2ft 9in (0.8m)
Displacement: 910 lbs (412kg)
Sail Area: 157 sq ft (14 sq m)
Designer: C. Raymond Hunt
Builders: Various

The prototype of the 110 was launched for the first time during the Marblehead Race Week in August 1939 when she proceeded to better the times of every other competing class except the 33ft International One-Designs.

The 110, designed by Raymond Hunt, is remarkable in a number of respects. Originally built in wood, but now more often in GRP, the overall length of the boat is greater than the height of its mast. The deck plan tapers from a beam of only 4ft 2in to a point at both bow and stern – leading to the quip that – 'Everything else is pointless.'

The hull has vertical flat topsides and a flat but slightly rockered bottom to which is bolted a 300 lbs iron fin keel – rather like a Flying Fifteen. It seems that before he came to design the 110, Ray Hunt had been greatly impressed by the performance of an amateur built canoe-stern centreboarder that had been designed by a German naval architect who had come to the US just before World War II. The amateur boat was 18ft overall and had 12 square metres

of sail, just like the International 12 Square-Metre Sharpie. As an experiment a temporary iron keel was fitted within the centreplate case and when the experiment proved successful, a second boat was built with a permanent fin keel. That was the boat that gave Hunt his idea for the 110.

The box like appearance of the 110 is often disguised by the use of clever paintwork.

'Working' sail area is 110 square feet, but with a roller furling genoa the permitted area now totals 157 square feet.

A 'bow-launching' 100 square foot spinnaker is also allowed; bow-launching referring to a self-draining tunnel in the foredeck.

A modern 110 is often equipped with the latest Harken fittings and Schaeffer spars, but only one set of new sails may be used each year.

In 1993, about fifty 110s were actively racing in the US; most of them in the Boston area, Michigan and Bay City. There are less active fleets at Rhode Island, San Francisco and Hawaii.

Most of the boats in the 110 (`One´-10) Class, like this one, are moulded in GRP.
Photo: Courtesy of Will Craig

Nordic Folkboat

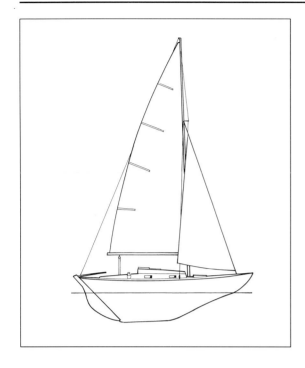

FB

Length Overall: 25ft 2in (7.64m)
Length Waterline: 19ft 8in (6.00m)
Beam: 7ft 3in (2.20m)
Draught: 3ft 11in (1.20m)
Displacement: 4255lb (1930 kg)
Sail Area: 260 sq ft (24 sq.m)
Designer: T Sunden
Builders: Various
Portsmouth Yardstick: 115

There are two versions of the origins of the Nordic Folkboat. In the British Folkboat Association's handbook, you will read that in 1939, some members of the Royal Gothenburg Yacht Club (the same Club that had already initiated the Dragon) felt that in addition to the Dragon, 6-metre and 8-metre classes, there was the need for a small inexpensive cruising boat that could also provide good racing. The idea was considered by the Swedish Yacht Racing Association and they decided to hold a competition for a suitable design. The competition drew almost sixty entries; none of which was considered entirely satisfactory. So a committee of three was formed – a Swede, a Dane and a Finn – and charged with combining the best features of the top four designs to create what would be the Nordic Folkboat.

Another version credits the idea to Sven Salen, head of the Salen Shipping Line and Commodore of the Royal Swedish Sailing Society in 1940. Salen is said to have told Tord Sunden, an amateur designer, about the disappointing results of the competition, whereupon Sunden offered a design for a 25ft clench-planked boat with a transom raked

at 45 degrees. Although concerned at first with the cut off stern, Salen liked the design and gained the support of the Swedish Sailing Society before proceeding to commission the building of a batch of sixty boats.

Which of these two accounts is correct may not matter, since whose-ever it was, the concept was sound and the Folkboat is well established, some 3,850 boats having been built during the half century of its history.

The Folkboat is 25ft 2in overall, 19ft 8in on the waterline, with a beam of 7ft 3in and a draught of 3ft 11in. The iron keel must not weigh more than 2350 pounds.

The first boat was built at Arendal in Sweden in 1942 and from the outset rules were drawn up to ensure a strict one-design class. Planking was of Swedish pine with stem, keel and deadwood of oak. The rig called for a tall solid wood mast, supported by a masthead backstay and a forestay attached at two-thirds of the height of the mainsail hoist. There is only a single shroud on either side and the combined sail area is 260 square feet.

Unbelievable as it may seem in 1992, when a new wooden Folkboat would probably cost

Skjoldunge was built by Sven-Erik Anderson in Sweden in 1962. Here, her owner,
David Freeman steers her through the Solent in 1992.
Photo: Ewan Joughin

£30,000, back in the early 1940s the first boats were sold in Sweden at the equivalent of £400 each.

It seems that Tord Sunden gained little from his contribution and some reports say that he was upset enough to bring actions against those who had paid him nothing for building from his plans. Eventually Sunden won an out of court decision that required builders to pay him 300 Kroner for each Folkboat they built.

Many clench-planked Folkboats were built in Britain by such yards as Parham of Emsworth, Woodnutts of Bembridge, Hamper of Fareham, Feltham and then Perry of Portsmouth and White of Brightlingsea.

The original Nordic Folkboat had simple week-end accommodation, comprising a couple of settee berths, a tiny galley and a bucket W.C. forward of the mast. Much better accommodation was built into many later Folkboats, including those made in East Germany and Poland, many of them having a larger coachroof and doghouse that together made them look very different from and less attractive than the original boat.

Some of the builders outside Scandinavia chose to use carvel rather than lap-strake construction and in 1949, Jim Saunders, a Lloyds surveyor, sought and obtained permission from the Scandinavian Class Association for British builders to use carvel construction for Folkboats.

Folkboats are raced as a one-design Class in Scandinavia, where the most coveted trophy is the Danish Gold Cup. But the British version is not one-design, since the rules allow considerable differences between boats. They can be either carvel or clench built, they can have larger than standard coachroofs as well as a doghouse and they are allowed inboard engines. So, Folkboats racing in the UK are divided into two sections – Open and Cruiser. The TCF for a boat with a fixed three-bladed prop is .806 and its Portsmouth Yardstick would be 124.

As the cost of building in wood increased, so the numbers of new Folkboats declined and as happened with so many other classes, a decision was made in 1975 to allow building in GRP. The hull of *Tibbe*, winner of the Gold Cup that year, was used to produce the mould from which the straked GRP Nordic Folkboat was produced, of which some 700 were sold in the decade that followed.

The hull lines of few other boats can have been 'borrowed' as often as those drawn by Tord Sunden for the Folkboat. Most of the derivatives, like the Invicta, the Contessa 26 and the Cutlass were built in GRP, although the Stella, Kim Holman's version of the Folkboat was clench built just like the original. The most famous boat to use a Folkboat hull must surely have been Blondie Hasler's *Jester*. This carvel-built junk-rigged boat competed in the first Singlehanded Transatlantic race back in 1960 and went on sailing back and forth across the Atlantic until 1986, when Michael Richey lost her after she was dismasted while lying ahull in a violent storm. A replacement replica of *Jester* was subsequently built by Peter Wilson at Aldeburgh and she was launched in 1992.

At least one Folkboat, Ann Gash's *Ilimo*, has been sailed singelhanded around the world, the story being told in 'A Star to Steer Her By'.

Photo Opposite:
The Folkboat *Sea Stride*, under spinnaker during the U.K. National Championship in the Solent in 1992. Photo: Malcolm Donald

Thistle One-Design

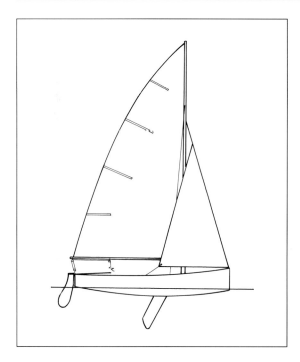

Length Overall: 17ft (5.2m)
Length Waterline: 17ft (5.2m)
Beam: 6ft 1.8m)
Draught: 9in (4ft 6in) –
(0.2m & 1.4m)
Displacement: 515 lbs (233kg)
Sail Area: 190 sq ft (17 sq m)
Builders: Various

Gordon, 'Sandy' Douglass, had built and sailed 14ft International dinghies in the US before World War II, and there is little doubt that he was influenced by the 14s when he came to design the 17ft Thistle, of which he said :

"She must be big enough to carry a large party in reasonable comfort, small enough to fit into the average small garage, light enough for two men to be able to lift her onto a trailer, and fast enough to give a good account of herself under all conditions. She must be reasonably dry and safer than the average. She must plane well and handle like a thoroughbred."

Douglass ensured that the Thistle would plane by giving her the same V sections forward and flat run aft that Uffa Fox had made famous with his 14ft Avenger in 1927.

Douglass launched the prototype on Lake Erie in the summer of 1945, taking part in an allcomers' handicap race over 15 miles. He was crewed by his wife and a beginner and recalls that there was 40 mph wind from the North-west and the seas: 'looked to be twelve feet high but probably not more than six or eight'. Other competitors included a large schooner and a 22-square-metre but the Thistles beat them all by a clear 20 minutes.

The first Thistles were built in wood, using the cold-moulding technique with several veneers applied at different angles but with the outer strips horizontal.

Like the International 14, the Thistle is undecked, with its mast stepped on a forward thwart. The centreplate is ballasted with 55lbs of lead. Sail area is 190 square feet, the same as an International 14, but no trapeze is allowed, so the Thistle is normally raced with a crew of three. There is also a 220 sq.ft spinnaker to keep the forward hands occupied.

The Thistle Class Association has more than a hundred fleets across in the US and some 4,000 boats have been built – most of them moulded in GRP in recent years. But the Class still proudly claims that – 'no change has ever been permitted that has obsoleted any older hull'.

The Thistle OD used to be described as a larger International 14, until that Class began to ship bowsprits. The Thistle certainly is an open boat and because she is 17 feet overall, a crew of three is needed most of the time.
Photo: Courtesy of the Thistle Class Association

National Firefly

F

Length Overall: 12ft (3.7m)
Length Waterline: 11ft 9in (3.6m)
Beam: 4ft 7in (1.4m)
Draught: 10in (3ft 9in)
- (0.2m & 1.1m)
Displacement: 550 lbs (249kg)
Sail Area: 90 sq ft (8.2 sq m)
Designer: Uffa Fox
Builder: Fairey Marine (until 1968)
Portsmouth Yardstick: 124

Even before the War, Uffa Fox was pleading with the International Yacht Racing Union to – *"foster and encourage one-design class racing"* because – *"the purpose of such a class is to make all the boats, their rigs and sails, as alike as possible, so that a man wins by his superior skill at sailing and the care he has taken to keep his boat in perfect condition."*

Despite such pleading, supporters of the one-design concept got little help from any of the official bodies until 1946, when the Yacht Racing Association adopted a design by Uffa Fox for a 12-foot moulded ply dinghy, with a beam of 4ft 8in.

The purpose of the Y.R.A. was to provide dinghy racing at the lowest possible cost and it was the novel method of hot-moulded ply construction that offered the opportunity to achieve that aim. The target price set for the first boats was £65, although that did not include sails.

The Firefly was an improved version of Uffa Fox's earlier Cambridge University One-Design, having flatter floors than either that dinghy or the Uffa King that had already proved a successful National 12-footer.

The Firefly was novel in several other respects. Firstly it was to be produced in quantity by hot-moulded plywood construction and secondly its spars were metal, the top section being tapered wood.

Initially the Y.R.A. intended to offer the Firefly with three optional rigs; a racing version with a total area of 89 sq ft; in jib and main; a gunter-rigged version with a total of 75 sq ft and a beginners rig using a small Bermudan main of only 50 sq ft set on a 14ft mast.

The boats were built by Fairey Marine Ltd., whose chairman was Major C.H.Chichester-Smith, a well-known International 14ft dinghy sailor. The original idea was that orders for the Firefly would be placed through local boatyards, who would get them from Fairey Marine at a discount. In the event and predictably, purchasers placed their orders direct.

The first Firefly was demonstrated at Henley-on-Thames in May 1946, when Charles Currey sailed her against some thirty National 12s for the Henley Open Challenge Cup. The Firefly, crewed by Mrs Chichester-Smith, won one of the heats and was second in two others. In the final race she was beaten only by the crack team of Jack Holt and

The first Firefly was demonstrated at Henley on Thames by Charles Currey in 1946, when she raced against a fleet of National 12 footers.

Given enough wind, Fireflies will plane, as this group of three is demonstrating on the river Crouch in the 1950s. Photo: Trevor Davies

Beecher Moore, sailing *Laughter*, their 12 foot National.

In 1948, two years after its introduction, the Firefly was chosen as the dinghy for the single-hander class at the 1948 Olympic sailing events in Torbay. It was there that the young Paul Elvstrom won the first of his several Olympic Gold medals. It was a week when there were strong winds and because the Firefly has a main and a jib, she often proved a handful and there were many capsizes. Elvstrom, who was lighter than the other helmsmen won the last and for him vital race, under a reefed main and a lowered jib. The lesson was learned and the Finn, with its single sail, was subsequently used for the single-hander event, which Elvstrom proceeded to win three more times.

Despite not being chosen a second time as an Olympic Class, the Firefly was a success as a two-man dinghy, particularly with University and Service sailing clubs where they were often used for team racing. Nevertheless there are some Firefly enthusiasts around who like sailing them single-handed and they still compete for the Single-Handed Championship.

In 1959, Terylene sails were permitted and in 1966 a Mark II Firefly was introduced with a revised deck layout but the same hull shape. In the following year an alloy centreplate was permitted to replace the heavier galvanised steel plate. Whether Uffa Fox would have approved this change might be questioned, since he had written – "*A steel centreboard has several advantages. When the boat is over at an angle of 45 degrees in a squall, the wooden centreboard tends to float up to the surface and capsize the boat. At this point however, the 45 lb steel drop-keel, because it tends to sink, is righting and not capsizing the boat*".

The most important change came in 1968, when it was decided to allow the Firefly to be built with GRP. A builder was appointed in 1972, and thus ended a quarter of a century's co-operation between the Class Association and Fairey Marine. The new GRP Firefly could have either a plastic or wooden deck and although built-in buoyancy was provided under the foredeck, buoyancy bags were used elsewhere. Masts underwent

a series of changes when it was no longer possible to obtain the composite wood and metal type originally used. First the change was made to an all metal spar that could still be rotated and then, in 1975, it was decided to accept a standard non-rotating mast that could be obtained anywhere.

In 1976, wooden boats began to be produced once again, this time cold-moulded by Knight and Pink Marine. This new version of the Firefly was designated the Mark III. It is claimed by the Association that the Firefly is one of the most strictly controlled one-design classes and remains so despite the numerous changes that have been made to keep the boats up-to-date and competitive. Although the rate of introduction of new boats had declined by the early 1990s, there were still some 3,500 registered Fireflies and some of the early Fairey Marine boats were still winning while others were being restored as classic one-designs, and early wooden boats were still winning. The 1992 National Championship, held at Tenby, was won by David Derby in F999, built in 1950.

Team racing in dinghies, which was introduced in this country in the 1930s, by Stewart Morris of the Oxford and Cambridge Sailing Society, began on the Broads in Yare and Bure One-Designs. But since 1948, Fireflies have been used and one of the most important events takes place each year at the West Kirby Sailing Club where teams compete for the Wilson Trophy

When he was fifty years old, Uffa Fox showed his confidence in the Firefly by sailing one through St Catherine's Race, to the South of the Isle of Wight in a near gale. He described the adventure in his book – 'Sailing Boats':-

"The fun and excitement of racing a light little 12-Footer like a Firefly under these conditions was more than I could resist and George Revell very kindly allowed me to steer his boat while he acted as crew. Out we went to win the afternoon race, with the finishing line to the western end of Ventnor. We were reaching in at a terrific speed to the finish line, when I suddenly said to George, 'What about saving the trouble of un-rigging, trailing to Shanklin and re-rigging there, by sailing home?' The prospect filled us both with glee, and so, directly we

received our winning signal we put out to sea again, to the amazement of the club on shore, because there was too much wind for us to shout our intentions ashore.

I did not lay her hard upon the wind, but took her off at an angle of some 50 degrees. This eased the wind pressure on our sail and increased our speed. It also meant that the waves were not coming at us as fast as they would at 45 degrees. In the hollow of the waves we sailed fast and serenely, and whenever we came to a breaking crest of the great big ones, we eased our sheets, and I bore away to take the sea on the beam, which meant that we were not contending with the wave, and the breaking crest could then wash us away to leeward. We were confident in this little boat as we knew that even if we swamped, she would quickly rise and shed the greater part of the water through her drop keel casing, while the buoyancy in her side tanks, coupled with the weight in her centreboard, would give her enough stability to jill along until we bailed the rest of the water out.

After an exhilarating and joyous sail, we came to the long flat sands of Shanklin with great seas and surf raging on them. We decided that as we arrived at the line of surf, George would leap over the side and run her through the breakers, at times shoulder high, while I lowered the sails. In we went with a swoop and so ended a wonderful day."

Dave and Nicky Derby, overall winners, at the start of one of the races for the Firefly National Championship in Pevensey Bay in 1991. Photo: Nick Champion

International 210 Class

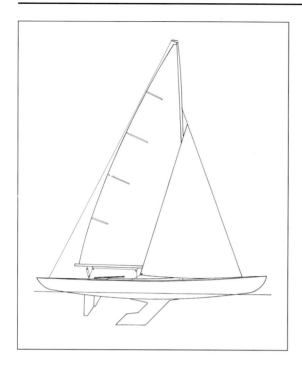

210

Length Overall: 29ft 10in (9.1m)
Length Waterline: 24ft (7.3m)
Beam: 5ft 10in (1.8m)
Draught: 3ft 10in (1.2m)
Displacement: 2300 lbs (1041kg)
Sail Area: 330 sq ft (30 sq m)
Designer: Raymond Hunt
Builders: Various

After Raymond Hunt had designed the fast and distinctive double-ended hard-chine 110 in 1939, he had many people asking – 'why not a larger boat than the 110 based on the same principles?' But it was not until 1945 that a group of members from clubs around Massachusetts Bay got together and commissioned Hunt to design a larger 110. The resulting boat was six feet longer than the earlier version, with 1ft 6in more beam and a slight but more attractive sheer. The first 25 boats were built in Graves yard at Marblehead and in those days they were made of plywood on steam-bent oak frames, an unusual form of construction for a hard-chine boat. Later, wooden boats were built using sawn frames for greater strength. Unlike the 110, the mast of the 210 is slightly longer than the overall length of the boat, which because of its narrow beam, requires a fin and bulb keel that weighs more than half the total displacement of the boat, to provide stability.

There is very little room in the cockpit of the 110 with its beam of little more than 4ft; so the larger cockpit of the 210 makes the boat a good deal more comfortable to sail, even with a crew of three.

During the 1940s, the 210 became the largest three-man keel-boat class in the U.S, and fleets were also established in Hawaii and the Philippines, giving the Class international status. But with the advent of new classes such as the Etchells 22, the popularity of the 210 waned for a time. This prompted the Association to introduce a number of changes designed to modernise the boat and its rig. The most significant decision, as it has been for many other one-design classes, was to allow boats to be built in GRP. The necessary change to the rules was made in 1967 and subsequently a number of other changes were made to permit the use of tapered alloy masts, roller furling headsails, spinnaker chutes, and in 1982, the use of Mylar sails. These changes have meant that some builders of 210s use balsa-cored GRP for their hulls and offer three different types of boat – Daysailer, Club Racer and Grand Prix – all of which comply with the Class rules.

In all, about 450 boats have been built, spread among 10 fleets, mostly located in the North East and Mid West.

The 210 gets its name from the 210 sq ft in its mainsail, which is augmented by a 120 sq ft genoa and a 320 sq.ft spinnaker. That much sail together with a modern cutaway fin keel and a 24ft waterline, makes the 210 a very fast boat. In fact it is the proud boast of the Class that the 210 beats boats like the International ODs, the Stars, the Solings and the J-24s when they meet each year at Marblehead.

Raymond Hunt, the designer, sailing the first 210 at Marblehead in 1946.
Photo: Courtesy of James Robinson

Aldeburgh Lapwing Class

Length Overall: 12ft 6in (3.8m)
Length Waterline: 11ft 9in (3.6m)
Beam: 4ft 8in (1.4m)
Draught: 8in (2ft 9in)
- (0.2m & 0.8m)
Sail Area: 100 sq ft (75 sq ft Junior)
(9.2 & 7.0 sq m)
Designer: Morgan Giles
Builder: Nunn Bros

In the letter from Peter Wilson that I mention in my introduction, he told me just how many one-design classes had been sponsored by the Aldeburgh Yacht Club at one time or another. Among those classes was a 12ft 6in lugsail dinghy called the Redwing, which was introduced around the turn of the century. Peter reckons that it must have been 'pretty horrible' and since there seems to be no record of its designer, he won't be upset by that view.

Morgan Giles designed two sail plans for the Aldeburgh Lapwing; a 'junior' rig with 75 square feet and the 'adult' with 100 square feet.

The Redwings survived for almost half a century, until they began to be replaced by another 12ft 6in, boat, designed by Morgan Giles in 1947. The Lapwing, as the new dinghy was called, has been described as a smaller version of the T.E.O.D. and E.O.D. that Giles designed soon after the Second World War. In 1922 he also designed the Dart OD which has dimensions that are similar to the Lapwing, although the earlier boat was gunter rigged, whereas the Aldeburgh was Bermudan from the start.

The Lapwings have a sail area of 100 sq ft when sailed by adults, but the Junior Lapwing carries only 75 sq ft when sailed by children.

The major change to the Class rules was made in 1954, when the old 75lb iron centreplate was discarded in favour of an alloy plate weighing 25lb.

Nunn Brothers of Waldringfield on the neighbouring river Deben, built most of the Lapwings; although a few were built by Appleyards of Lincoln for the Ely Sailing Club, but as Peter Wilson reports, they have all ended up at Aldeburgh. More recently a couple of Lapwings have been built by local yards, bringing the total to 73.

Today, most of the youngsters manage to handle the larger area of sail. This shot was taken during the Aldeburgh Week Regatta in 1989. Photo: Coloryan

International Cadet

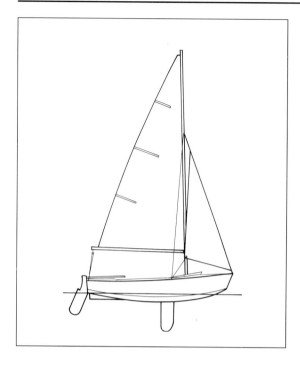

Length Overall: 10ft 6œin (3.2m)
Length Waterline: 9ft 3in (2.8m)
Beam: 4ft 2in (1.2m)
Draught: 6½in (2ft 6in)
- (0.16m & 0.76m)
Displacement: 120 lbs (hull) (54kg)
Sail Area: 55 sq ft (5 sq m)
Designer: Jack Holt
Builders: Various
Portsmouth Yardstick: 152

In 1945, immediately after the War, Group Captain Edward Haylock became editor of 'Yachting World', the well known British yachting periodical. One of the first things he did was to have Jack Holt design a dinghy that would be easier to build and cheaper than an International 14. The result was the Merlin, a 14ft restricted class dinghy, the plans of which were published in the January 1946 issue of 'Yachting World'.

The success of the Merlin prompted Haylock to sponsor a dinghy that would appeal to youngsters under the age of 18. This time Jack Holt came up with a 10ft 6in hard-chine sailing pram that could be built with the water-resistant plywood that had become available after the War. To make things easier for the amateur builder and for any company prepared to sell the dinghy in kit form, the angle between the floor and the gunwale remained the same throughout the length of the boat. The Cadet is three-quarter decked and its buoyancy is provided by airbags or in compartments that must be proved to be substantially water-tight before the boat can be registered.

Everything about the boat was kept as simple as possible. A dagger-plate was chosen instead of a swivelling centreboard; lanyards were used instead of rigging screws and a fixed rudder with a lifting blade enabled the boat to be launched off a beach ready to sail away.

Explaining his reasoning and purpose, Edward Haylock said:

"The number of clubs in England that did anything for young people could be counted on the fingers of one hand; while the type of boat normally given to children to sail was usually uninteresting to say the least of it. As a rule they had just a lug-sail and had few claims to be nice to handle. There were all sorts of odd theories, the chief of which was that the boat must be open, to teach the children not to capsize. The majority had little or no proper buoyancy and were heavy for youngsters to haul about on the beach.

What I wanted to do was give youngsters something which not only looked like father's boat, but which also had a really good performance. She had to be safe and suitable also for general knockabout purposes as well as for racing."

From the outset the Cadet was intended for a crew of two and in order to keep both of

The Royal Corinthian YC (their clubhouse is in the background), has hosted the annual Cadet Week since the earliest days of the Class. This race would have been circa 1960. Photo: Trevor Davies

them busy, there are main, jib and spinnaker sails to hoist and trim. Haylock was particularly keen on giving the boat a spinnaker because he felt that: "... *spinnaker drill is by no means a strong point even in our crack classes, and this, I am sure is because neither helmsmen nor crews have grown up to regard the spinnaker as a normal and essential part of the equipment of a racing boat.*"

Inclusion of a spinnaker in the sail plan of the Cadet gave rise to opposition in some clubs, who questioned the wisdom of encouraging youngsters to handle a spinnaker in such a small dinghy. But Haylock always stuck to his guns and insisted that children would soon learn how to deal with a spinnaker under all conditions. That he was right was shown in 1965, when the Class rules were changed to allow a larger spinnaker.

The hard-chine double-transom design of the Cadet was so unusual at the time that

no orthodox boatbuilder seemed to be interested in it. However, quite by chance, 'Dusty' Miller of the Bell Woodworking Company happened to spot the prototype on its trailer outside a hotel in Farnham. While examining it Haylock and Holt emerged from the restaurant and the three of them got into a conversation that concluded with a promise to send Miller a set of plans.

About a month after that Miller turned up at 'Yachting World' with a complete set of parts and fittings that could be sold for less than £40. Until then Bell Woodworking had been making bee-hives!

Just as the Snipe had thrived on the back of the American magazine 'Yachting', so the Cadet owed much of its early popularity to the publicity it received through the pages of 'Yachting World', while Group Capt. Haylock remained its editor.

Some very successful helms have started in a Cadet.
Photo: Coloryan.

Jack Holt's plans were first published in the September '47 issue and within a few months it was obvious that the boat would be popular in many countries outside the UK.

It also became clear that if the Cadet was to be successful as a Class, then some kind of controlling body would be necessary. So the Yachting World Cadet Class Association was formed, with Group Capt. Haylock as President and Peter Scott as Vice-President and Secretary. A simple set of rules were drawn up with an emphasis on safety.

In 1949, the Y.W. Cadet was granted recognition by the Y.R.A.; yet to become the Royal Yachting Association. By 1950 there were enough Cadets around in the UK to justify holding the first national Regatta and at the invitation of 'Tiny' Mitchell, Commodore of the Royal Corinthian YC, the meeting was held at Burnham-on-Crouch in Essex. That first year there were only forty four entries but a precedent was established and Cadet Week, as it was called thereafter, became the highlight of the year for generations of Cadet owners and their crews.

The success of these early regattas was largely due to the practical support given by such people as Charles Curry, Jack Holt, Beecher Moore, Peter Scott, Gerald Sambrooke-Sturgess, and of course Edward Haylock himself. In 1958 the Cadet was granted International status by the IYRU and by 1965 some 3,500 Cadets had been built world-wide, with more than a hundred different fleets (squadrons) established. This growing international importance of the Class led to a separate UK National Cadet Class Association being formed in 1966, leaving the Central Committee to deal with the separate member countries and World Championships.

Over the years, Cadet World Championship meetings have been held once or more in Canada, Poland, Spain, Australia, Yugoslavia, Belgium, Portugal, Italy, Holland, India, Turkey, Argentina, Hungary, and the UK. There has never been an International meeting in Russia, although by 1968 some 3,000 unregistered boats had been built in the USSR which represented the largest fleet in the world.

Poland on the other hand has been the stronghold of the Eastern Europeans, led by their champion Jerzy Borowski, who won six of the World Championship races at Whitstable in 1971, only to be disqualified from all the races because 'his boat was shallower than the rules permitted'. An indication of the strictness with which the one-design requirements have been enforced.

Not many changes were made to the Class rules during the 1950s and 60s but in 1957 frameless construction was allowed, which made it easier and cheaper for Cadets to be produced in quantity. Amateurs continued to build on frames and the new rules ensured that a frameless boat was no more likely to win than an amateur built Cadet. In fact during Cadet Week some years later, the top ten places were taken by equal numbers of framed and frameless boats. Cotton sails were regulatory until 1959, after which, 'any woven cloth' could be used. Rigging lanyard, chosen in the first place for economy and safety because they could be cut to release a mast in emergency, were standard until the 1980s, after which rigging screws allowed easier and better adjustment of rig tension. Metal masts were allowed after 1960, but were not generally adopted before 1970, when light 'bendy' spars became available.

By the mid 1960s, the Central Committee had to face the fact that the number of new boats was beginning to decline and that several countries were calling for a relaxation of the rule requiring all boats to be built of wood. In 1967 the Committee decided that Cadet hulls 'may be made of any materials suitable for marine construction'. Even then there was no rush to build in GRP and it was 1971 before a moulded boat won the National Championship.

There is little doubt that adopting new materials and allowing the use of modern gear, made the Cadet more attractive to youngsters who might otherwise have been tempted by other, more stylish, dinghies. However, these changes did result in a professionally built Cadet costing more, so that by 1992 as much as £2,400 was being asked for a Mk III Cadet.

Some famous yachtsmen, including Rodney Pattissen and Chris Law, have sailed Cadets, but only one – John Wilshire – has sailed a Cadet across the English Channel to Cherbourg and back; a feat no doubt admired if not approved by his parents and the officers of the National Cadet Association.

International Optimist

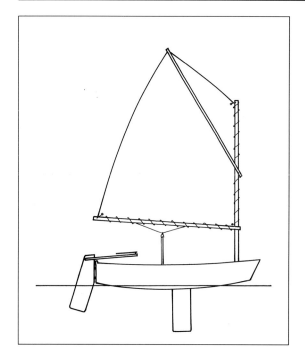

Length Overall: 7ft 7in (2.3m)
Length Waterline: 7ft (2.1m)
Beam: 3ft 8Ωin (1.1m)
Draught: 3in (2ft 6in)
– (7.6cm & 0.76m)
Displacement: 77lbs (35kg)
Sail Area: 35 sq ft (3.2 sq m)
Designer: Clark Mills
Builders: Various
Portsmouth Yardstick: 174

It is appropriate that the last boat to be discussed is the smallest and the most numerous of all the one-design classes.

It has been estimated that more than 250,000 Optimist dinghies have been built, many of them by their owners, since the first one was launched in 1947.

There are some remarkable similarities between the origins of the Optimist and those of the Cadet. It seems that in 1947, the year in which the Cadet was launched, Major Cliff McKay, a retired US Army Officer, decided that his local Optimist Club should start a – 'kids' training program.' So he turned to a designer named Clark Mills for help in producing – 'a simple little boat that a boy and his dad could build for $50.'

Clark Mills found that in the US at that time he couldn't buy plywood sheets longer than 8 feet, so he drew a boat with an overall length of only 7ft 7in. He also decided that if he used a spritsail, all three spars could be made from cheap and easily obtained curtain poles and could be stowed in the boat. The sail itself was flat-cut from 6 ounce drill material.

Initially there were few rules to be observed; simple limits to overall length and beam and

a condition that the boats were intended for children no more than 15 years old.

The aims were modest and Clark Mills remembers remarking that 'If we can just teach six kids sailing, it's worth it.'

The impetus that eventually led to the Optimist becoming the largest International Class came from a Dane. In 1959 Axel Damgaard was in the US where he saw an article in a yachting magazine describing the 'Optimist Pram'. Like Haylock, McKay and Mills before him, Damgaard believed that youngsters needed a cheap and simple boat in which to learn to sail, so he took plans of the Optimist back to his local sailing club at Vordingborg, 70 miles south of Copenhagen.

The club quickly approved the idea that five boats should be built and within a very short time, interest spread and Optimists were being built all over Denmark.

In 1957 popularity of the Class received a further boost when Olympic champion, Paul Elvstrom gave the Optimist his support by helping at summer schools and regattas, so that by 1960 there were more than 2,000 Optimists sailing in forty Danish clubs.

Further expansion came in 1960, when the Englishman Nigel Ringrose, sailed his 16ft

Shearwater catamaran to the Baltic and the eastern coast of Denmark. By chance he put into Vordingborg, where the Optimist had been introduced six years earlier. While windbound, Ringrose was surprised to see a number of children happily sailing their Optimists in the strong wind. He was so impressed that after returning to England, he imported a Danish-built Optimist and lent it to his nine-years-old cousin, Davina Sheridan, to sail on the Hamble. Next, Ringrose and his mother set up a company to build Optimists commercially and then established the Optimist Class Racing Association based in his grandmother's house at Bursledon.

At first, progress was slow, but the mother and son team persisted and in 1960 they organised the first Optimist meeting to be held in the UK. The venue was Bursledon on the Hamble and things were kept simple because as the organiser said: –

"The Class Association appreciates that most participants will have little or no knowledge of racing rules and no previous racing experience. However, the following Class Rules will be strictly observed:-

At least two separate buoyancy units, together supporting at least 100 pounds, must be securely fitted to the boat.

All participants in races must wear life-jackets."

Encouraged by the modest success of that first meeting, (there were 12 entries) Nigel Ringrose decided to organise the first International Regatta for Optimists in 1962. He invited Optimist Associations in Denmark, Sweden and West Germany to send four or five children each to compete against a British team.

Because of their greater experience in the Class, the Danes and Swedes were able to teach their hosts a great deal and it was not surprising that the series was won by Anders Quiding from Sweden while second place was taken by the Dane Peder Due, who was to win a silver medal in the Tornado class at the 1980 Olympic Games.

Nigel Ringrose had always seen the Optimist as an international boat and with that aim in mind the International Optimist Dinghy Association was formed during the 1965 Regatta at Turku in Finland.

Throughout the 1960s the popularity of the Optimist grew steadily until by the end of that decade, there were fleets in Argentina, Belgium, Denmark, Finland, France, Greece, Morocco, Norway, Rhodesia, Spain, Sweden, Turkey, the UK, the USA, West Germany and Yugoslavia.

Not unreasonably these countries sought IYRU recognition, which was granted in 1973. At that time, the RYA, which had been somewhat indifferent to the Optimist until then, also recognised the Class and by 1980 their opinion of the Optimist had changed enough for them to make it their official single-handed junior training boat. In the UK, Optimist sailing was confined to the Solent area for most of the 1960s, but thereafter fleets began to appear all around the coast as well as on inland waters, so that during the 1980s, some 200 clubs had Optimists and in that decade the National Championship was won by boats from as far apart as Weston SC, Draycote Water SC and the Hayling Island Optimists.

As with most other successful one-design classes, much deliberation took place before the International Optimist Association decided to allow boats to be built in GRP. After several 'experimental' hulls had been made and exhibited, official approval was given in January 1970 – 'provided the GRP boats were not inferior to a wooden boat in respect to safety, strength and buoyancy'. Even after that a serious problem arose in 1974, when it was found necessary to scrap or re-build 1,000 GRP boats that did not comply with the measurement rules because the bottom of the bow transom was 30 mm too high.

Wooden construction continued – particularly by amateurs, some of whom have produced some beautiful Optimists.

The Optimist is small, its rig is basically simple and the rules ensure that it remains a true one-design class. But none of this has prevented enthusiasts from devising ways to make an Optimist go faster, as can be seen from the information and advice given in a brochure from a company supplying Optimist gear.

"The Optimist is one of the smallest racing boats in the World, and also one of the most hotly contested. All measurements are restricted and strictly enforced, but there

This Optimist was one of the first to be built in the U.K. and was still being sailed in 1992. This photograph, taken in 1969, shows Richard Clampett at the helm during the Optimist National Regatta in Stokes Bay. Photo: Eileen Ramsey

A young Dutchman sailing his Optimist in the Open and National Championship races off Harwich in 1990. Photo: Coloryan

are some equipment advantages and tuning techniques which can help to improve boatspeed.

The Optimist is a good carrier of weight with its flat bottom, and for competitive racing, crew weight ranges from 38kg to 52kg. As a general rule a lighter crew will have softer spars with a flat sail and a heavier crew will have stiffer spars with fuller sails.

Setting up the mast correctly is important, and you need to identify three different mast rake positions using the adjustable mast step.

Sprit adjustment is the most important consideration in the rig. The sail will normally have creases radiating from the head, and these are trimmed out by increasing tension on the sprit adjuster.

The sprit should be adjusted on every point of sailing for best performance.

Make sure the outhaul is calibrated, it will only be necessary to release the clew in medium wind conditions, to increase power, otherwise it is set for maximum spread. The kicking strap is left slack for light airs – under about 6 knots. Above this wind strength apply enough kicker to stop the leech twisting.

Sailing upwind in heavy winds it may be necessary to de-power the boat. Make sure you are on maximum rake and then try raising the centreboard by 3-4 inches, angling the bottom aft and the top forward."

An Optimist with a good racing record could fetch as much as £1,500 in 1992 – a far cry from the boat with curtain pole spars built by Clark Mills for $50, back in 1947.

Optimists today are a far cry from the $50 boat that Clark Mills built back in 1947.
Photo: Coloryan

Index